Seoul in 3 Days – Travel Guid

Welcome to the ultimate guide to Seoul, the vibrant and dynamic capital city of South Korea! Seoul is a bustling metropolis that offers a unique blend of traditional Korean culture and modern urban living. From its ancient palaces and temples to its trendy shopping districts and lively nightlife, Seoul has something to offer every traveler. Whether you're a foodie, a history buff, or just looking to experience something new, Seoul is sure to captivate you.

In this guide, we'll take you through all the must-see attractions and hidden gems of Seoul. We'll explore the best neighborhoods, hotels, restaurants, and shopping districts, as well as provide tips on navigating the city, dining etiquette, and cultural customs. You'll also find information on day trips and excursions, as well as practical advice on staying connected, staying safe, and getting the most out of your Seoul adventure.

So, buckle up and get ready to discover all the wonders that Seoul has to offer!

Contents

Seoul in 3 Days – Travel Guide 1
I. Introduction 3
   A. Welcome to Seoul 3
   B. A Brief History of Seoul 4
   C. The Culture and People of Seoul 7
   D. The Best Time to Visit Seoul 9
   E. Currency and Language 11
II. Getting to and Around Seoul 14
   Traveling to Seoul 14
   Getting to Seoul from Gimpo Airport 14
   Getting to Seoul from Incheon Airport 17
   A. International Airports 21
   B. Transportation Options 22
   C. Navigating the City 24
III. Accommodations 27
   Detailed Guide to Seoul Neighborhoods 27
   A. Hotels 29
   B. Guesthouses and Hostels 36
   C. Unique Stays 39
   D. Our Recommended Budget Stay 41
   E. Frequently Asked Questions about Staying in Seoul 43
IV. Sightseeing 46
   A. Historical Sites 46
   B. Modern Attractions 47
   C. Parks and Nature 48
   D. Museums and Cultural Centers 49
   E. Off-the-Beaten-Path Attractions 50
V. Shopping 53
   A. Shopping Districts 53

- B. Markets 53
- C. Malls and Department Stores 54
- D. Specialty Shops and Souvenirs 56
- E. Tips for Shopping in Seoul 56

VI. Food and Dining 58
- A. Traditional Korean Cuisine 58
- B. Street Food 63
- C. Themed Cafes and Unique Dining Experiences ... 64
- D. International Cuisine 65
- E. Vegetarian and Vegan Options 66
- F. Tips for Dining in Seoul 67

G. Mini Guide to Coffee Shops in Seoul 69

VII. Nightlife 71
- A. Neighborhoods for Nightlife 71
- B. Bars and Clubs 71
- C. Live Music and Performances 72
- D. Cultural Performances and Shows 73
- E. Karaoke Bars 75
- F. Rooftop Bars 76

VIII. Day Trips and Excursions 76
- A. The DMZ and Panmunjom 76
- B. Nami Island 77
- C. Suwon Hwaseong Fortress 78
- D. Everland Theme Park 79
- E. Jeonju Hanok Village 80

IX. Travel Tips and Safety 81
- A. Staying Connected: Wi-Fi and SIM Cards 81
- B. Etiquette and Cultural Tips 81
- C. Emergency Contacts and Useful Apps 83

Fun Things to Do in Seoul 84

- Explore Korean Palaces and Traditional Markets 84
- Enjoy Night Views of Han River and Namsan Tower 85
- Hike Bukhansan Mountain a 85
- Taste Endless Korean Food 86
- Late Night Shopping in Seoul 87
- Gorgeous Photoshoot in Hanbok 88

Seoul Mountains: 89
- Bukhansan National Park 89
- Seoul Fortress Wall Hike 92

3-Day Seoul Classic Travel Itinerary 97
- 1st Day in Seoul: 97
- 2nd Day in Seoul: Seoul Fortress Wall 104
- 3rd Day in Seoul: 112

Thank you 117

I. Introduction

A. Welcome to Seoul

Welcome to Seoul, the vibrant and dynamic capital city of South Korea! With a rich history dating back over 2,000 years, Seoul is a unique blend of ancient traditions and cutting-edge modernity. As a global economic powerhouse and a hub for technology, fashion, and entertainment, Seoul draws millions of tourists each year, captivated by its bustling street markets, grand palaces, and world-class shopping districts.

The city's skyline is a fascinating mix of ancient temples, traditional hanok houses, and ultra-modern skyscrapers. Seoul's charm lies in its ability to harmoniously combine these diverse elements, offering visitors a multitude of unforgettable experiences. From exploring serene Buddhist temples and wandering through charming historic neighborhoods to enjoying the pulsating nightlife and indulging in mouth-watering Korean cuisine, there is something for everyone in this exciting city.

In this comprehensive guide, we'll help you navigate Seoul's rich offerings, providing insider tips and detailed information to make the most of your visit. So pack your bags, and let's embark on an unforgettable journey to the heart of South Korea. Welcome to Seoul!

Introduction

Seoul (Seoul Special Metropolitan City) is the capital of the Republic of Korea (also known as South Korea) and the largest city in the country. Seoul Capital Area (Sudokwon) includes Incheon City, Gyeonggi-do (province surrounding capital) and Seoul making it the fifth largest metropolitan area in the world. About 50% (51 mln) of South Korea's population live in Seoul Capital Area, and around 10 mln people live in Seoul alone. The area is mountainous and has an average elevation of 38 m (125 ft). Seoul was established during the Baekje Kingdom (18 BC-660 AD) as a capital Wiryesong. The modern name Seoul has been used since 1882 together with its other names such as Hanseong, Hanyang, Gyeongseong or Keijo. Most of the time in Korea's history, Seoul served as the main capital city.

Photo of Seoul from Seoul Fortress Wall hike

Winter in Seoul can be cold with an average temperature drop to -15 C. Spring and fall have pleasant weather as the temperature is perfect for staying outdoors. Expect humid summer with monsoon starting from late June and lasting till late July. July is the hottest month of the year.

The architecture of Seoul can be easily described as a divert or 'where the modern meets traditional' as there are a lot of traditional buildings and old neighborhoods next to modern tall buildings. This scenery is widely loved by tourists.

The view of Seoul: where modern meets traditional

All year round Seoul is famous for its street food that variety depends on the season. The most famous street food is *ddeokbokki* (spicy rice cake) that is a representative of Korean street food. On a street vendor, you can find *hotteok* (sweet pancake), *kimbap* (seaweed roll with ham and vegetables), *odeng* (fish cake) and other types of Korean food. Street food is easy to find as its smell fills all the streets.

Korean traditional alcohol is very simple and doesn't have much selection. The most famous drinks are soju (weak vodka) and makgeolli (rice wine). These drinks have a wide selection of flavors such as original, grape soju, peach makgeolli, citrus soju and etc. It is very popular to drink in the public while having a gathering between friends near the river or in the park.

Jogyes a Temple in the middle of Seoul

B. A Brief History of Seoul

The history of Seoul, South Korea's thriving capital, is a captivating tale of resilience, growth, and transformation. Spanning over 2,000 years, Seoul's journey has seen it rise from an ancient fortress city to a modern metropolis and global hub. To understand the soul of Seoul, let's delve into its fascinating past.

Founding and the Three Kingdoms Period (57 BCE - 668 CE)

Seoul's origins can be traced back to the establishment of Wiryeseong, the capital of the Baekje Kingdom, around 18 BCE. Located near the Han River, Wiryeseong served as a strategic stronghold during the Three Kingdoms Period, which saw the Korean Peninsula divided among the rival kingdoms of Goguryeo, Baekje, and Silla. This period of intense rivalry contributed to the development of unique arts, culture, and architecture in each kingdom.

The Unified Silla and Goryeo Dynasties (668 - 1392 CE)

In 668 CE, the Silla Kingdom, allied with the Tang Dynasty of China, managed to conquer both Goguryeo and Baekje, unifying the Korean Peninsula under the Unified Silla Dynasty. The capital was moved to Gyeongju, with Wiryeseong losing its significance. However, this era saw the spread of Buddhism, which profoundly influenced the culture and architecture of the region.

The Goryeo Dynasty, founded in 918 CE, succeeded the Unified Silla Dynasty. Although the capital was located in modern-day Kaesong, Seoul remained an important regional center. The Goryeo Dynasty is particularly notable for the creation of the Tripitaka Koreana, an extensive collection of Buddhist scriptures that showcase the kingdom's prowess in woodblock printing.

The Joseon Dynasty and Hanyang (1392 - 1897 CE)

The Joseon Dynasty marked a new era for Seoul. Founded in 1392, the dynasty moved the capital from Gaegyeong (Kaesong) to Hanyang, the former site of Wiryeseong, in 1394. Hanyang, known today as Seoul, flourished under the dynasty's rule, becoming the political, economic, and cultural center of Korea.

During the early Joseon period, the city's layout was meticulously designed, with the grand Gyeongbokgung Palace at its heart. The city was encircled by a massive defensive wall, with the four main gates, Namdaemun, Dongdaemun, Seodaemun, and Bukdaemun, guarding its perimeters. The Joseon Dynasty saw a Confucian-inspired cultural renaissance, marked by numerous advancements in science, literature, and the arts.

Unfortunately, the 16th and 17th centuries brought instability and strife as the Japanese invasion (1592-1598) and the Manchu invasions (1627 and 1636) wreaked havoc on the city. The city's palaces, including Gyeongbokgung and Changdeokgung, were severely damaged, and thousands of lives were lost. However, the resilient people of Seoul rebuilt the city, restoring its cultural and architectural treasures.

The Korean Empire and Japanese Occupation (1897 - 1945)

As the Joseon Dynasty weakened, Korea's last king, Gojong, proclaimed the founding of the Korean Empire in 1897, with Seoul as its capital. This era witnessed rapid modernization, as Western-style buildings, transportation, and communication systems were introduced to the city. However, the Korean Empire was short-lived, as Japan annexed Korea in 1910, marking the beginning of a 35-year occupation.

The Liberation and Postwar Reconstruction (1945 - 1960)

With the surrender of Japan at the end of World War II in 1945, Korea was liberated from Japanese colonial rule. In the aftermath, the Korean Peninsula was divided into two zones, with the United States administering the southern half and the Soviet Union the northern half. This division eventually led to the establishment of the Republic of Korea (South Korea) in 1948, with Seoul as its capital.

The Korean War (1950-1953) between North and South Korea devastated the country and left Seoul in ruins. The city changed hands multiple times during the conflict, causing significant damage to its infrastructure, cultural heritage, and population. After the signing of the armistice agreement in 1953, which established the Korean Demilitarized Zone, South Korea focused on rebuilding and modernizing Seoul, with the help of international aid.

The Miracle on the Han River (1960 - 1990)

South Korea experienced rapid economic growth from the 1960s to the 1990s, a period known as the "Miracle on the Han River." The country transformed from an agrarian society into an industrial powerhouse, with Seoul at the forefront of this remarkable development. During this time, the city underwent extensive urban planning and construction, which led to the expansion of its boundaries and the creation of new infrastructure, such as highways, bridges, and subways.

Seoul's population exploded, as people from across the country flocked to the city in search of better opportunities. The cityscape began to take on a more modern appearance, with the construction of high-rise buildings and the development of new neighborhoods.

The 1988 Summer Olympics, held in Seoul, showcased the city's progress on the international stage and further boosted its economic growth.

The 21st Century: A Global City (1990 - Present)

Seoul entered the 21st century as a global city, boasting advanced technology, a diverse cultural scene, and a high standard of living. The city has continued to evolve, with a focus on sustainability, green spaces, and innovative urban design. Landmark projects, such as the restoration of the Cheonggyecheon Stream and the construction of the Dongdaemun Design Plaza, highlight Seoul's commitment to balancing modernity with its historical and cultural heritage.

Today, Seoul is a thriving metropolis and a major player in the global economy. As a hub for technology, fashion, and entertainment, the city attracts millions of tourists each year who come to explore its rich history, vibrant culture, and world-class amenities.

The history of Seoul is a testament to the resilience and determination of its people. Through countless challenges and transformations, the city has emerged as a dynamic and thriving metropolis that is proud of its past and ready to embrace its future. As a visitor, you'll have the opportunity to immerse yourself in Seoul's captivating history and create your own memories in this remarkable city.

C. The Culture and People of Seoul

Seoul, as the heart and soul of South Korea, is a melting pot of rich traditions, diverse influences, and modern trends. The culture and people of Seoul are the product of a fascinating historical journey, blending ancient customs with contemporary ideas to create a unique identity that defines this vibrant metropolis.

Traditions and Customs

The people of Seoul, like the rest of South Korea, have deep-rooted Confucian values that emphasize family, respect for elders, and social harmony. Age hierarchy and social etiquette play an important role in daily life. Bowing is a common way to greet or show respect, and addressing others by their titles or surnames is customary.

Seoul's residents also take pride in their traditional arts and crafts. Pottery, calligraphy, and embroidery are just a few examples of the centuries-old crafts that are still practiced and appreciated today. Traditional dance and music performances, such as pansori (a form of musical storytelling) and samulnori (percussion music), can be enjoyed at various cultural events throughout the year.

Language

The official language of Seoul is Korean, which uses the Hangul script. Developed in the 15th century during the Joseon Dynasty, Hangul is a unique phonetic alphabet that is relatively easy to learn. Although English is taught in schools and spoken by many, especially in tourist areas, it is helpful to learn a few basic Korean phrases to facilitate communication and show respect to the locals.

Fashion and Style

Seoul has emerged as a global fashion capital, with cutting-edge designs and a thriving street fashion scene. The city's style-savvy residents have a penchant for mixing high-end brands with local designs, creating unique and bold looks. Neighborhoods like Myeongdong, Hongdae, and Gangnam are popular shopping destinations for fashion enthusiasts.

Traditional Korean attire, known as hanbok, is still worn by locals during special occasions, such as weddings and national holidays. Visitors can also rent hanbok and explore the city's palaces and historic sites, adding a touch of cultural immersion to their experience.

Food and Culinary Traditions

The people of Seoul take great pride in their culinary heritage, which boasts a diverse array of flavors and ingredients. Traditional Korean meals often center around rice, vegetables, and fermented dishes, such as kimchi. Bulgogi (marinated grilled beef), bibimbap (mixed rice with vegetables and meat), and tteokbokki (spicy rice cakes) are just a few examples of the mouth-watering dishes you'll encounter in Seoul.

The city's food scene also includes vibrant street food markets, such as Gwangjang Market and Myeongdong Street Food Alley, where you can sample local favorites like hotteok (sweet pancakes) and odeng (fishcake skewers). Seoul's thriving cafe culture and international cuisine options also reflect the city's cosmopolitan spirit.

Contemporary Culture and K-Pop

Seoul is the epicenter of the global K-Pop phenomenon, a genre of music that combines catchy tunes, energetic performances, and visually stunning music videos. The city is home to major entertainment companies, such as SM Entertainment, YG Entertainment, and JYP Entertainment, which have produced internationally acclaimed artists like BTS, BLACKPINK, and EXO. The influence of K-Pop extends beyond music, shaping fashion trends, beauty standards, and even language.

In conclusion, the culture and people of Seoul are a fascinating amalgamation of history, tradition, and contemporary influences. As a visitor, you'll have the unique opportunity to immerse yourself in this vibrant tapestry, gaining a deeper understanding of the city's spirit and creating lasting memories of your time in the South

D. The Best Time to Visit Seoul

Seoul offers a unique experience in every season, with distinct weather patterns, festivals, and events throughout the year. Deciding on the best time to visit Seoul depends on your preferences for weather, attractions, and activities. Let's explore the advantages and drawbacks of each season to help you choose the perfect time for your trip.

Spring (March - May)

Spring in Seoul is a magical time, as the city comes alive with cherry blossoms, azaleas, and other vibrant flowers. The mild temperatures, ranging from 5°C (41°F) to 22°C (72°F), provide a pleasant environment for outdoor activities and sightseeing. This season is perfect for strolling through parks, such as Yeouido Hangang Park or Namsan Park, to witness the stunning blooms and enjoy picnics with friends and family.

Spring is also a time for various festivals, including the Yeouido Cherry Blossom Festival and the Lotus Lantern Festival, which showcase the city's cultural heritage and natural beauty. The downside to visiting during spring is that it can be crowded with tourists and locals alike, who flock to enjoy the blossoming season.

Summer (June - August)

Summers in Seoul can be hot and humid, with temperatures often climbing above 30°C (86°F). While the weather might not be ideal for everyone, the city offers numerous indoor attractions and air-conditioned spaces to escape the heat. During the summer months, the Han River becomes a popular destination for water sports, such as kayaking, and for leisurely evening strolls.

Summer is also the season of various music and arts festivals, such as the Seoul International Cartoon and Animation Festival and the Seoul Fringe Festival. Be aware that the monsoon season, which typically occurs from late June to late July, can bring heavy rain and occasional thunderstorms, so be prepared with appropriate rain gear.

Autumn (September - November)

Autumn is another favorite season for travelers visiting Seoul. The crisp air and comfortable temperatures, ranging from 8°C (46°F) to 25°C (77°F), make it ideal for exploring the city's many outdoor attractions. The vibrant fall foliage, with shades of red, orange, and yellow, paints the city's landscapes, especially in the mountains surrounding the city, such as Bukhansan National Park and Seoraksan National Park.

Autumn also offers several cultural events, including the Seoul International Fireworks Festival and the Korea International Art Fair. The downside of visiting during autumn is that it can also be a busy tourist season, so you may need to book accommodations and attractions in advance.

Winter (December - February)

Winter in Seoul can be cold and dry, with temperatures often dropping below freezing. However, the city's snow-covered landscapes and festive atmosphere during the holiday season can be enchanting. If you're a fan of winter sports, this season provides an opportunity to visit nearby ski resorts, such as Vivaldi Park and Yongpyong Resort.

Winter also sees fewer tourists, which means that popular attractions might be less crowded, and accommodation prices may be lower. It's essential to pack warm clothing and be prepared for icy conditions during this season.

In conclusion, the best time to visit Seoul depends on your personal preferences for weather, activities, and crowd levels. Spring and autumn are the most popular seasons for their mild temperatures and natural beauty, while summer and winter offer unique experiences and fewer crowds. Regardless of the season, Seoul is sure to captivate you with its charm and endless attractions.

E. Currency and Language

Navigating a foreign city can be both exciting and challenging, especially when it comes to understanding the local currency and language. To help make your trip to Seoul as smooth as possible, here's what you need to know about South Korea's currency and language.

Currency

The official currency of South Korea is the Korean Won (KRW). Banknotes come in denominations of 1,000, 5,000, 10,000, and 50,000 won, while coins are available in 10, 50, 100, and 500 won denominations. It's essential to familiarize yourself with the local currency to ensure smooth transactions and avoid confusion when making purchases.

Credit cards are widely accepted in Seoul, including at hotels, restaurants, and shopping centers. However, it's always a good idea to have some cash on hand for smaller establishments, street food vendors, and local markets that may not accept cards. ATMs are readily available throughout the city, and many of them offer services in English and other languages. Be aware that some ATMs might charge a withdrawal fee, so it's best to check with your bank before your trip.

Currency exchange services can be found at banks, hotels, and specialized currency exchange booths. The best exchange rates are often found at banks, but it's essential to compare rates at different locations to get the best deal. It's advisable to exchange a small amount of money before arriving in Seoul, just in case you need cash immediately upon arrival.

Language

The official language of Seoul is Korean, which uses the Hangul script. Developed in the 15th century during the Joseon Dynasty, Hangul is a unique phonetic alphabet that is relatively easy to learn. Korean grammar and sentence structure are different from English, so learning the basics might take some time, but a little effort goes a long way in making your trip more enjoyable and immersive.

English is taught in schools, and many locals, especially in tourist areas and among younger generations, can speak and understand it to some extent. However, fluency in English is not universal, and it's helpful to learn a few basic Korean phrases to facilitate communication and show respect to the locals. Here are some useful phrases to get you started:

- 안녕하세요 (Annyeonghaseyo) – Hello

- 감사합니다 (Gamsahamnida) – Thank you

- 실례합니다 (Sillyehamnida) – Excuse me

- 네 (Ne) – Yes

- 아니요 (Aniyo) – No

- 얼마예요? (Eolmayeyo?) – How much is it?

- 영어를 할 줄 아세요? (Yeongeoreul hal jul aseyo?) – Do you speak English?

In addition to English, some locals may speak other languages, such as Chinese or Japanese. You'll also find that signs, menus, and maps in popular tourist areas are often available in English, Chinese, and Japanese, making it easier for international visitors to navigate the city.

To further assist with communication, consider downloading a translation app or carrying a pocket-sized phrasebook with you during your trip. These resources can help bridge the language gap and ensure that your experience in Seoul is as enjoyable and hassle-free as possible.

II. Getting to and Around Seoul

Traveling to Seoul

Traveling by plane is the most convenient and quickest way to reach South Korea. There are many direct and transferring flights from various countries all over the world. Most famous airlines are Asiana Airlines, British Airways, Korean Air, KLM, Emirates, Aeroflot, Lufthansa, and Finnair. However, you can choose any other airlines depending on your budget and the country you are flying from.

Seoul has two international airports – Gimpo and Incheon that are out of Seoul Metropolitan City but belong to Seoul Capital Area. Below you will find details about both airports and ways to travel to Seoul.

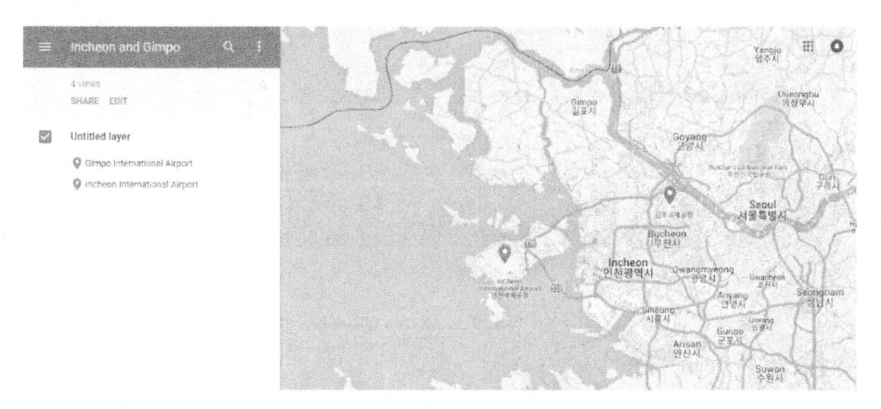

Get this map online: https://goo.gl/fFuHDw

Getting to Seoul from Gimpo Airport

Gimpo Airport is technically still in Seoul, however, you can find it quite farm from the main districts of Seoul. Gimpo Airport is the oldest airport in South Korea as it was established in 1939 as an airfield for the Japanese Army and in 1958 Gimpo became an international airport. It is a small airport that has two small terminals for domestic and international flights. Most of the flights from and to Gimpo is domestic flights. However, there are a few airlines that other great deals flying to Gimpo airport. Take a look below to get more information about transportation from Gimpo to Seoul.

1.) Getting to Seoul by subway

The most convenient way is to take a subway line to get to your accommodation. There are many signs leading to the subway and ticket vending machines. The best way to save money on the subway is to buy a T-money card that costs around 2500 won (around $2.5). You have to top up with the wanted amount of money. More about the T-money card you can find here: https://english.visitkorea.or.kr/enu/TRP/TP_ENG_8_1_1.jsp.

a.) Seoul Subway Line 5 – starting subway price with T-money card will be 1250 won ($1.2) for the first 10 km and will increase by 100 won ($0.1) for every additional 5 km. This line goes across Seoul with a few main stops at the Seoul downtown and major tourists' attractions. Map of the line: https://www.airport.co.kr/uploads/CONTENTS/site/gimpoeng/subway_line5.png

b.) Seoul Subway Line 9 – starting price will be 1250 won ($1.2) and will increase by 100 won ($0.1) for every additional 5 km. This line goes across the southern part of Han River and has an express subway that skips minor stops. Perfect for those who are staying at the southern part or for transferring to different lines. Map of the line: https://www.airport.co.kr/uploads/CONTENTS/site/gimpoeng/subway_line9.png

c.) AREX – it is a special subway that is called Airport Railroad Express: express train and all stop train. Gimpo Airport only operates 'all stop train' as 'express train' only departs from Incheon Airport. 'All stop train' usually costs around 1450 won ($1.45) to go to the last stop at Seoul station (around 15 min or less). However, if you are transferring, as your accommodation is on a different line, the price can drop or increase. Map of the line: https://www.airport.co.kr/uploads/CONTENTS/site/gimpoeng/subway_line9.png

2.) Getting to Seoul by bus

Using a bus can be more complicated and more expensive than subway depending on where you are going and what kind of bus you have decided to use.

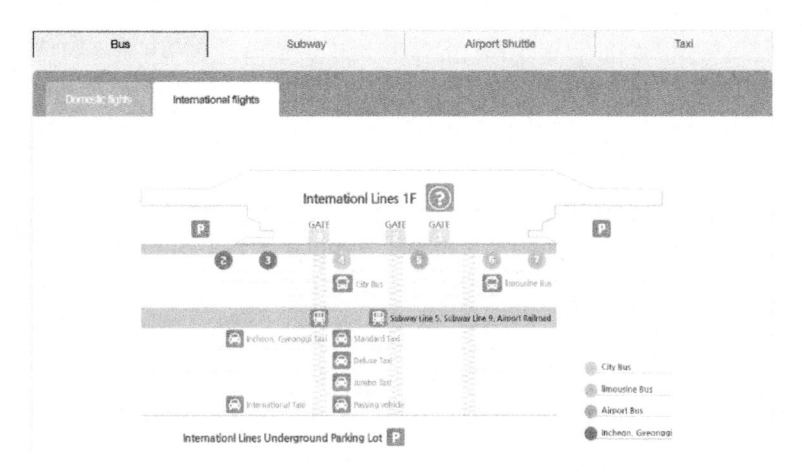

Map of Gimpo Airport bus station. International flights side

a.) City bus – this bus goes around Seoul and you can use a T-money card on it. Prices vary from 1250 won ($1.25) to 2500 won ($2.5) if you are paying by T-money card. If you are paying by cash, add an extra 100 won ($0.1) to the card price. **Remember!:** you have to press the bell if you want to get off. More information: https://www.airport.co.kr/gimpoeng/extra/bus/busList/layOut.do?menuId=1834&categoryIdx=2

b.) Limousine bus – this bus is more like a comfortable coach that has plenty of space for luggage. Limousine bus takes you to major stops in Seoul so you can comfortably reach your accommodation. Prices vary from 4000 won ($4) to 7500 won ($7.5). You can find more information here: https://www.airport.co.kr/gimpoeng/extra/bus/busList/layOut.do?menuId=1834&categoryIdx=3

3.) Getting to Seoul by taxi

Getting a taxi is cheap in Seoul and it's the best way to travel if you don't wish to use public transportation. There are different types of taxi and the starting price is also different for them. In order to identify the type of taxi, you can refer to the map above.

a.) Standard taxi – starting price for the first 2 km is 3000 won ($3). You will get charged a 100 won ($0.1) for every additional 142 m. Every orange and silver taxi is a standard taxi.

b.) Deluxe taxi – starting price is 5000 won ($5) for the first 3 km. You will get charged a 200 won ($0.2) for every additional 164 m. Deluxe taxis are usually black and are more luxury than a standard taxi.

c.) International taxi – drivers of international taxi are fluent in a foreign language such as English, Japanese or Chinese. They have standard and deluxe taxis, and prices are slightly higher than regular taxis.

You can find more information at Gimpo Airport website: https://www.airport.co.kr/gimpoeng/content/contents.do?cid=2016010811264189412&menuId=1837

A very useful general guide of Seoul taxis: http://english.visitseoul.net/essential-Info-article/Taxi_/16758

Getting to Seoul from Incheon Airport

Incheon airport is the largest airport in Seoul and South Korea. Several times it was rated as one of the best airports in the world. Recently a second terminal was added to the airport. Incheon Airport is located on the island of Incheon Metropolitan City that belongs to Seoul Capital Area, so it's completely outside Seoul and has various ways to reach Seoul.

1. Traveling to Seoul from Incheon Airport Terminal 1 and Terminal 2

Please, refer to the maps below for the guidance of finding a way to transportation.

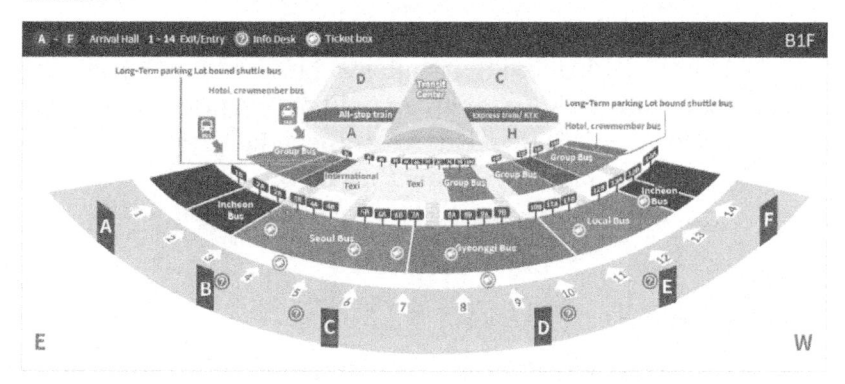

Map of Incheon Airport Terminal 1 public transportation

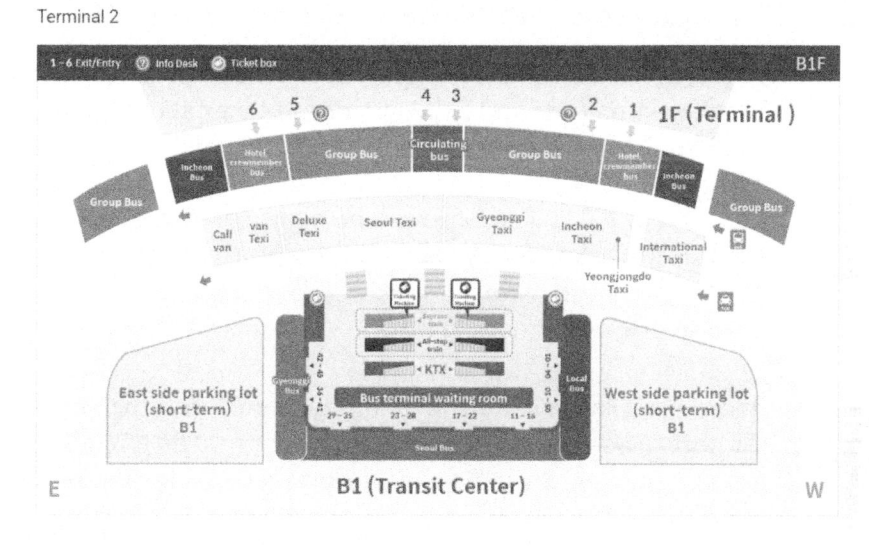

Map of Incheon Airport Terminal 2 public transportation

a.) By bus

You can purchase tickets at the ticket box (shown in the map) or use T-money card – transportation card that can be purchased at the vending machine/convenience store in the airport for around 2500 won ($2.5). You will need to top up before using.

- **Seoul City buses:** go to major Seoul districts and easy to reach almost every part of Seoul. The usual fare starts from 10 000 won ($10) to 16 000 won ($16). You can check all the fares and

21

times here:
https://www.airport.kr/ap/en/tpt/busRouteList.do
- **Late night buses:** two routes of late-night buses are: Seoul Station bound and Gangnam bound. The fare is 9000 won ($9). Very convenient if you arrive at Incheon Airport late at night. More information and times are here:
https://www.airport.kr/ap_lp/en/tpt/pblctpt/pblctpt1/pblctpt1.do

b.) By AREX

AREX is an Airport Railroad Express that has two kinds of subway trains: 'all stop train' and 'express train'. It can be the cheapest way to travel from Incheon Airport to any part of Seoul. Don't forget to get a T-money card as you can save some money by using it.

- **All Stop Train:** this subway train is connected to the major Seoul destinations and subway lines. It takes about 59 minutes to go to the last station – Seoul station. The usual price for this train is 4150 won ($4.15) from Terminal 1 and 4750 won ($4.75) from Terminal 2. The price can be higher or lower depending on your destination and transfers. More information about fares:
https://www.arex.or.kr/content.do?url=&menuNo=MN20 1503300000000008&contentNo=&clientLocale=en_US&clientDevice=Normal
- **Express Train:** a nonstop train that runs from Incheon Airport to Seoul station in less than 50 min. The fare is 9000 won ($9). Also, you can enjoy various benefits for Express train users. This way of traveling is the best if you need to reach Seoul comfortable. More information:
https://www.arex.or.kr/content.do?url=&menuNo=MN20 1503300000000001&contentNo=&clientLocale=en_US&clientDevice=Normal

Useful more detailed information about AREX can be found here:
http://english.visitkorea.or.kr/enu/TRP/TP_ENG_2_1.jsp

c.) By taxi

Seoul taxi is quite cheap compared to another big city. There are a few different types of taxis and their prices are slightly different and you will get charged additionally to every 100 meters.

- **Standard taxi:** base fare is 3000 won ($3), additional charge for every 142 meters is 100 won ($0.1). Standard taxi colors are orange and silver.
- **Deluxe taxi:** base fare is 5000 won ($5), additional charge for every 164 meters is 200 won ($0.2). Deluxe taxi is more luxury, larger and comes in black color.
- **International taxi:** drivers can speak any foreign language written on their car. The base fare is usually the same as a standard taxi, however, an additional charge can be more expensive. Usually, international taxi charge more than they should do, so be careful to pay a little bit more than expected.

Take a look at Incheon Airport website for additional information about taxi: https://www.airport.kr/ap/en/tpt/pblcTptTaxi.do

Useful travel information:

- Visit Korea website:
  http://english.visitkorea.or.kr/enu/index.jsp
- Travel Hotline: 1330 (Korea), +82 2 1330 (from overseas)
- Incheon Airport help desk: 1577-2600, +82 2 1577 2600 (from overseas)
- Renting a SIM card:
  https://roaming.kt.com/rental/eng/main.asp

Banks: Monday to Friday, from 9 AM to 4 PM. KEB bank offers off-hours services and 365-day banking. ATM services open around 8.30AM and close around 10 PM. Some of the ATMs will be open until midnight. The best option to take out money is during the daytime.

Credit Cards: Every store accepts credit card, however, check with your bank about additional charges.

GMT: GMT +9

A. International Airports

Seoul is served by two major international airports: Incheon International Airport (ICN) and Gimpo International Airport (GMP). These airports connect Seoul to numerous destinations worldwide, making the city easily accessible to international travelers.

Incheon International Airport (ICN)

Incheon International Airport, located approximately 50 km (31 miles) west of Seoul, is the primary gateway to South Korea and one of the busiest airports in the world. It has consistently been ranked among the best airports globally, known for its excellent facilities, services, and cleanliness.

The airport has two main passenger terminals, Terminal 1 and Terminal 2, with several airlines offering flights to and from destinations across Asia, Europe, North America, and Oceania. Incheon International Airport also serves as a hub for major South Korean airlines, such as Korean Air and Asiana Airlines.

Transportation options from Incheon International Airport to the city center include the Airport Railroad Express (AREX), buses, taxis, and private transfers. The AREX train is the fastest and most efficient way to reach central Seoul, taking approximately 43-53 minutes, depending on whether you choose the express or all-stop service.

Gimpo International Airport (GMP)

Gimpo International Airport, located about 15 km (9 miles) west of central Seoul, is the city's secondary airport. Although it primarily serves domestic flights, it also offers international connections to select destinations in China, Japan, and Taiwan.

Gimpo International Airport is smaller and closer to the city center than Incheon International Airport, making it a convenient option for travelers flying within the region. Transportation options from Gimpo International Airport to central Seoul include the Seoul Metropolitan Subway, buses, taxis, and private transfers. The subway is the most convenient and affordable way to reach the city center, with Line 5 and Line 9 connecting the airport to various parts of Seoul.

When planning your trip to Seoul, consider your travel itinerary and preferred transportation method when choosing between Incheon International Airport and Gimpo International Airport. Both airports offer excellent facilities and services, ensuring a comfortable and hassle-free arrival experience.

B. Transportation Options

Seoul offers a convenient and efficient transportation system that makes getting around the city a breeze. From the subway and buses to taxis and bicycle rentals, there are various options to suit your travel needs and budget. Let's explore each of these transportation options in detail.

Subway

The Seoul Metropolitan Subway is a reliable and affordable way to travel around the city, with 21 lines serving over 600 stations. The subway operates from around 5:30 am to midnight, with trains running every 3-10 minutes, depending on the line and time of day.

To use the subway, you need to purchase a T-money card, which can be bought at most convenience stores and subway stations. The card costs 4,000 won ($3.50) and can be recharged with any amount of money. Alternatively, you can purchase single-use tickets from vending machines at the subway stations. These tickets are slightly more expensive than using the T-money card, and you will need to buy a new ticket for each ride.

The subway system has both Korean and English signage and announcements, making it easy for tourists to navigate. You can also download apps like Subway Korea or Kakao Metro to plan your route, check the train schedules, and receive real-time updates on any delays or disruptions.

Buses

Seoul has an extensive bus network that connects various parts of the city. The bus system includes local and express buses, with fares ranging from 1,200 won ($1) to 2,200 won ($1.80), depending on the distance traveled and the type of bus.

To pay for your bus fare, you can use your T-money card or purchase a single-use transportation card on board the bus. The bus system has both Korean and English signage and announcements, but it can be more challenging to navigate than the subway, especially for tourists. However, several apps, such as Seoul Bus or Naver Maps, provide information on bus routes and schedules, making it easier to plan your route.

Taxis

Taxis are readily available in Seoul and offer a convenient way to get around the city, especially for short trips or if you're carrying heavy luggage. There are two types of taxis in Seoul: regular taxis, which are colored silver or white, and deluxe taxis, which are black with a yellow stripe.

Regular taxis charge a base fare of 3,800 won ($3.30), with additional charges based on the distance traveled and time spent in traffic. Deluxe taxis have a higher base fare of 5,000 won ($4.30) but offer more spacious and luxurious interiors.

To hail a taxi, you can either wait at a taxi stand or flag one down on the street. You can also use ride-hailing apps like Kakao T or Uber to book a taxi in advance or for a specific location. Taxis have meters that show the fare, and tipping is not customary in South Korea.

Bicycle Rentals

Seoul offers several bicycle rental services, with bike stations located throughout the city. These services provide a fun and eco-friendly way to explore Seoul's many sights and attractions.

One of the most popular bike rental services in Seoul is Ttareungyi, which has over 400 bike stations and more than 20,000 bikes available for rent. To use Ttareungyi, you need to download the app, register for an account, and add money to your wallet. The rental fee is 1,000 won ($0.87) for the first hour and 500 won ($0.43) for each additional hour.

Another bike rental service is Seoul Bike, which has around 150 bike stations and offers both electric and regular bikes. To use Seoul Bike, you need to purchase a prepaid card or use a credit card at a rental station, then select your bike and start riding. The rental fee for Seoul Bike is 1,000 won ($0.87) for the first 30 minutes and 500 won ($0.43) for each additional 30 minutes.

When using bike rental services, it's essential to follow traffic rules and ride safely. Seoul has designated bike lanes in many areas, and riders are required to wear helmets. Some rental services also provide helmets, but it's best to bring your own if possible.

Tips for Getting Around Seoul

- Plan your route ahead of time: Research your destination and transportation options before your trip to save time and avoid getting lost.

- Use transportation apps: Download apps like Subway Korea, Seoul Bus, or Kakao T to help plan your route, check schedules, and receive real-time updates on delays or disruptions.

- Consider transportation passes: If you plan to use public transportation frequently, consider purchasing a transportation pass, such as the T-money card or Seoul City Pass, to save money and make transportation more convenient.

- Be aware of rush hour: Avoid traveling during rush hour, which typically occurs from 7:30-9:30 am and 5:00-7:00 pm, to avoid crowded trains and buses.

- Carry cash and small bills: Some transportation options, such as buses or taxis, may only accept cash, so it's always a good idea to carry some with you.

- Be respectful: When using public transportation or hailing a taxi, be courteous to other passengers and drivers, and follow local customs and etiquette.

C. Navigating the City

Navigating a new city can be both exciting and daunting, especially if you're unfamiliar with the language, culture, and transportation options. However, with a bit of preparation and knowledge, exploring Seoul can be a smooth and enjoyable experience. Here are some tips to help you navigate the city:

Familiarize Yourself with the City's Layout

Seoul is a vast city, but its transportation system is well-connected and easy to use. Before your trip, take some time to familiarize yourself with the city's layout, major landmarks, and transportation options. You can use online maps, travel guides, or smartphone apps to plan your route and find points of interest.

Seoul is divided into 25 districts or "gu," each with its own unique attractions and experiences. Some of the most popular districts for tourists include Jongno-gu, Gangnam-gu, and Myeong-dong. Jongno-gu is home to many historic sites, such as Gyeongbokgung Palace and Bukchon Hanok Village, while Gangnam-gu is known for its modern skyscrapers, luxury shopping, and nightlife. Myeong-dong is a bustling shopping district with many street vendors and trendy shops.

Use Public Transportation

Seoul has an extensive public transportation system that includes subways, buses, taxis, and bicycles. The subway system, in particular, is fast, reliable, and affordable, with trains running every few minutes. You can use a T-money card to pay for your fares, which can also be used on buses and some taxis.

Buses are another convenient option for getting around Seoul, especially if you're traveling to destinations that are not directly served by the subway. Taxis are readily available and can be hailed on the street or via smartphone apps like Kakao T or Uber. Bicycle rentals are also available at many locations throughout the city.

Learn Basic Korean Phrases

While many Koreans speak English, learning some basic Korean phrases can help you navigate the city more easily and show respect to the locals. Some useful phrases include:

- 안녕하세요 (annyeonghaseyo) - Hello

- 감사합니다 (gamsahamnida) - Thank you

- 실례합니다 (sillyehamnida) - Excuse me

- 여기 어디에 있어요? (yeogi eodie isseoyo?) - Where is this place?

- 지하철역 어디에 있어요? (jihacheolyeok eodie isseoyo?) - Where is the subway station?

Use Smartphone Apps

Smartphone apps can be a useful tool for navigating Seoul, whether you need help with directions, translations, or recommendations. Some popular apps include:

- Subway Korea: A subway map and route planner for the Seoul Metropolitan Subway system.
- KakaoMap: A GPS-based map app that provides driving and walking directions, real-time traffic updates, and public transportation information.
- Naver Translate: A translation app that supports Korean and many other languages.
- Visit Seoul: An official travel guide app for Seoul, with information on attractions, events, and restaurants.

Stay Safe

Seoul is generally a safe city, but it's always essential to take precautions when traveling. Keep your valuables secure and be aware of your surroundings, especially in crowded areas or at night. It's also a good idea to follow local customs and etiquette, such as removing your shoes before entering a Korean-style restaurant or home.

III. Accommodations

Detailed Guide to Seoul Neighborhoods

We have made a small guide to Seoul neighborhoods with a great selection of accommodation for your short stay in Seoul. However, Seoul has 25 districts with lots of different kinds of neighborhoods and all of them offer places to stay, so if you don't like our selected neighborhoods, you can easily find another one that is more suitable for you. Find all districts' map here: http://bit.ly/2IwLcHv

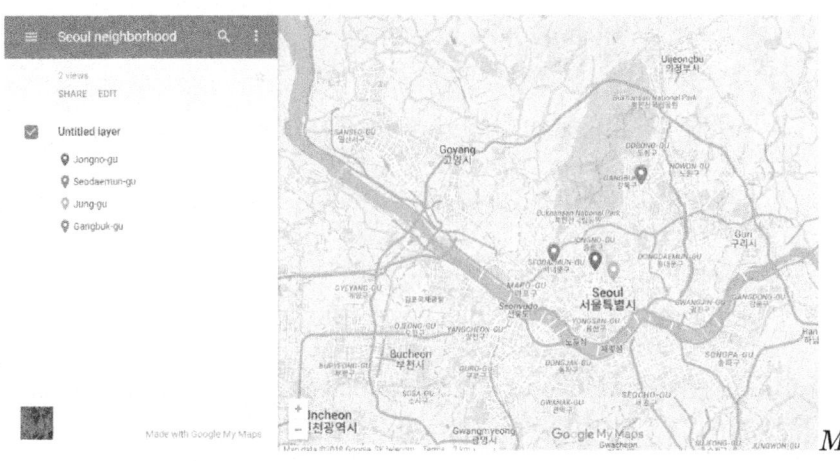

Map of neighborhoods. Get the map: http://bit.ly/2rGtvuP

#Jogno-gu

Jogno district is in the center of Seoul and has historic value as it is surrounded by five royal palaces, traditional Korean houses, museums, temples, and current presidential residence. Jogno is a great example of 'where the modern meets traditional' as next to traditional buildings you will be able to spot tall buildings, luxurious hotels, and department stores. To be added, Jogno holds major tourists attractions and can be easily explored on foot or by subway. There are many options to stay in Jogno no matter what kind of budget you are traveling. Buam-dong, Samcheong-dong, and Gahoe-dong offer great traditional hanok guesthouses. Prices start from 50 000 won ($50) per night for a double room. Breakfast is always included in a room rate. If you wish to stay in a luxurious hotel with a great view, Jogno has numerous 4-star and 5-star hotels that will guarantee you an amazing stay. However, if you are traveling on a budget, Hyehwa-dong and Ihwa-dong have various nice youth hostels and guesthouses for under 20 000 won ($20) for a private room. Also, these two neighborhoods are filled with cheap great restaurants, pubs, shops, Korean students and great parks with amazing views.

#Seodaemun-gu

Seodaemun district is next to Jogno district and offers various types of accommodation and close to popular places of Seoul. Seodaemun has several luxurious hotels that can be found around Chungjeongno-dong near Seodaemun subway station. The less expensive accommodation is located near Sinchon-dong that is home of famous Korean universities like Yonsei, Hongik, Ehwa, and Sogang. Sinchon-dong is great not only for low priced hostels but also for shopping and nightlife. North side of Seodaemun has lots of Airbnb apartments and rooms with a great rate, so it's worth to check them out as Seodaemun is the inexpensive place, close to major attractions and offers a great view of mountains.

#Jung-gu

Jung district is another central Seoul district that is connected with Seodaemun-gu and Jogno-gu. The district has various historic objects including Seoul Station and Namdaemun, main busy streets and tall modern buildings. Also, it's the main spot for tourists to stay in Seoul as the district is filled with various hostels, guesthouses and amazing hotels for a very decent price. If you are looking for something classy but cheap, head to Myeong-dong for great deals on hotels, hostels, and guesthouses. Myeong-dong is a busy neighborhood where you can enjoy nice restaurants, great nightlife, and never-ending shopping. If you wish for something more luxurious and historical, Taepyeongno-dong has a famous Koreana Hotel that was built in 1969 and has a marble lobby. It's a 4-star hotel with a very good price range as prices per queen room start from 70 000 won ($70). However, you can always grab a deal for a simpler room.

#Gangbuk-gu

Gangbuk-gu is located further in the North of Seoul. All Neighborhoods in this district are very quiet with lots of great views of mountains and parks. Gangbuk-gu is suitable for people who want tranquility and be surrounded by nature. Mia-dong and Suyu-dong have great guesthouses and nice AirBnB apartments that fit really nicely with the atmosphere. If you are planning to stay in Gangbuk-gu, take into account that you will have to be on a bus or subway for quite a lot of time if you want to reach major tourists destinations.

A. Hotels
1. Luxury Hotels

Seoul is home to a wide range of accommodations, from budget-friendly hostels to luxurious five-star hotels. If you're looking for a bit of pampering during your stay, there are plenty of luxury hotels to choose from. Here are some recommendations:

a) Four Seasons Hotel Seoul

Located in the heart of the bustling Gwanghwamun district, the Four Seasons Hotel Seoul is a luxurious five-star hotel that offers unparalleled comfort and service. The hotel features 317 spacious rooms and suites, each equipped with modern amenities such as flat-screen TVs, iPod docking stations, and Nespresso machines.

The hotel's facilities include a rooftop garden, indoor and outdoor pools, a fitness center, and a spa that offers a range of treatments. The hotel's Michelin-starred restaurant, Yu Yuan, serves exquisite Cantonese cuisine, while the Boccalino restaurant offers Italian fare. The hotel's convenient location is just steps away from Gyeongbokgung Palace, the National Museum of Modern and Contemporary Art, and several subway stations.

Average price: $500-$700 per night

Website: https://www.fourseasons.com/seoul/

b) The Shilla Seoul

Nestled in the scenic Seokchon Lake area, The Shilla Seoul is a luxurious hotel that offers stunning views of the city and the surrounding mountains. The hotel features 464 well-appointed rooms and suites, each with its own unique style and design.

The hotel's facilities include several restaurants and bars, a fitness center, an indoor pool, and a spa that offers traditional Korean treatments. The hotel's location is ideal for exploring the nearby Lotte World amusement park, the Olympic Park, and the Jamsil Sports Complex. The hotel is also close to several subway stations, making it easy to access other parts of the city.

Average price: $300-$500 per night

Website: https://www.shillahotels.com/seoul/en/main.do

c) Park Hyatt Seoul

The Park Hyatt Seoul is a luxurious hotel that offers panoramic views of the city skyline and the nearby Namsan Mountain. The hotel features 185 elegantly furnished rooms and suites, each with modern amenities such as flat-screen TVs, Bose sound systems, and complimentary Wi-Fi.

The hotel's facilities include a fitness center, an indoor pool, and a spa that offers a range of treatments. The hotel's restaurant, The Lounge, serves international cuisine, while the Timber House bar offers Korean-style tapas and cocktails. The hotel is located in the trendy Gangnam district, close to several subway stations and the COEX Convention & Exhibition Center.

Average price: $300-$500 per night

Website: https://www.hyatt.com/en-US/hotel/south-korea/park-hyatt-seoul/selph

Below you can find some more picks:

Lotte Hotel Seoul in Jung-gu: https://booki.ng/2IfHUoG

Lotte Worl Hotel in Songpa-gu: https://booki.ng/2wzr0jj

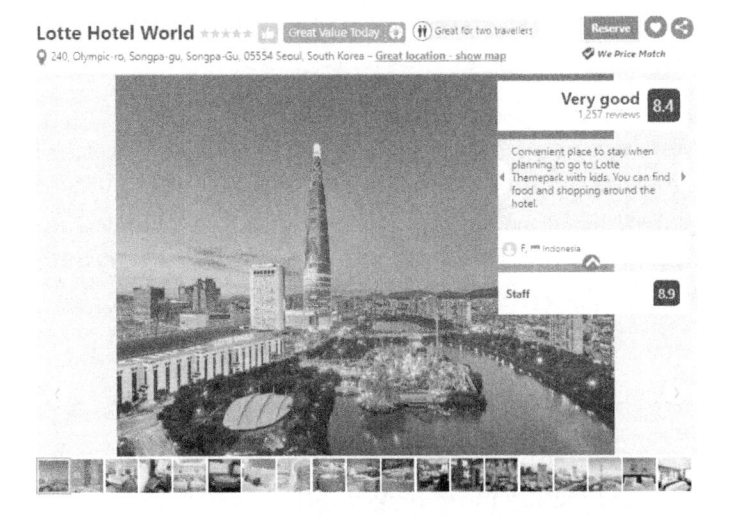

InterContinental Seoul COEX in Gangnam-gu: https://booki.ng/2IDvwm1

InterContinental Seoul COEX in Gangnam-gu:

Grand Mercure Ambassador Seoul in Yongsan-gu: https://booki.ng/2rD1EeW

The Plaza Seoul in Jung-gu: https://booki.ng/2rDOtLB

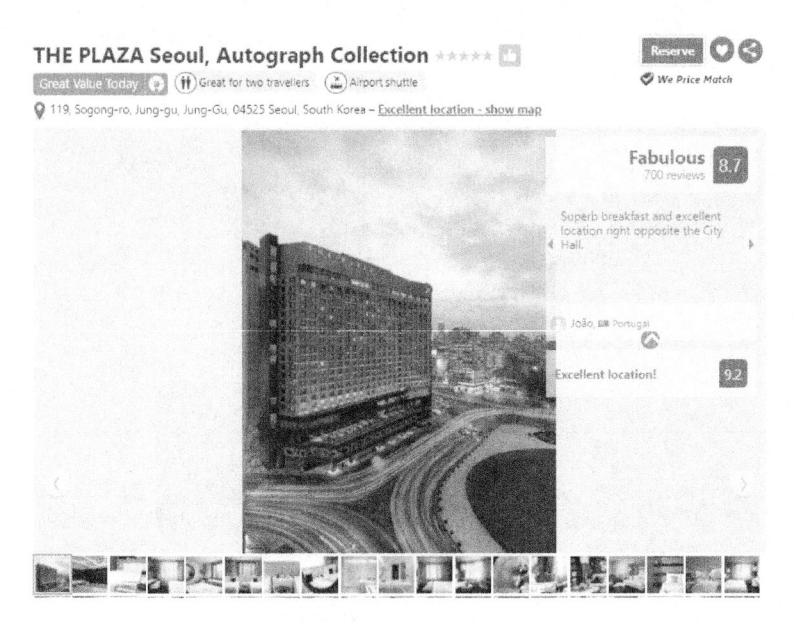

Millennium Seoul Hilton in Jung-gu:
https://booki.ng/2KWPNB2

Four Seasons Hotel Seoul in Jongno-gu:
https://booki.ng/2wDKBPq

2. Mid-range Hotels

a) Hotel28 Myeongdong

Located in the popular Myeongdong shopping district, Hotel28 Myeongdong is a stylish hotel that offers modern rooms and suites. The hotel's 136 rooms feature minimalist design with floor-to-ceiling windows, flat-screen TVs, and Nespresso machines.

The hotel's facilities include a fitness center, a rooftop terrace, and a lounge area with free snacks and drinks. The hotel's location is perfect for exploring Myeongdong's shops, restaurants, and street food stalls, as well as nearby attractions like Namsan Tower and the Gyeongbokgung Palace.

Average price: $100-$200 per night

Website: https://www.hotel28.co.kr/myeongdong/

b) Loisir Hotel Seoul Myeongdong

Loisir Hotel Seoul Myeongdong is a modern hotel located in the heart of Myeongdong. The hotel's 600 rooms feature contemporary design with amenities such as flat-screen TVs, minibars, and free Wi-Fi.

The hotel's facilities include a fitness center, a rooftop garden, and several restaurants and cafes, including a bakery and a rooftop bar. The hotel is within walking distance of Myeongdong's shops, restaurants, and street food stalls, as well as the Namsan Tower and the Gyeongbokgung Palace.

Average price: $80-$150 per night

Website: https://www.loisirmyeongdong.com/en/

c) Tmark Grand Hotel Myeongdong

Tmark Grand Hotel Myeongdong is a contemporary hotel located in the heart of Myeongdong. The hotel's 576 rooms feature modern design with amenities such as flat-screen TVs, minibars, and free Wi-Fi.

The hotel's facilities include a fitness center, a sauna, and several restaurants and cafes, including a bakery and a rooftop bar. The hotel's location is ideal for exploring Myeongdong's shops, restaurants, and street food stalls, as well as nearby attractions like the Gyeongbokgung Palace and the Namsan Tower.

Average price: $80-$150 per night

Website: https://www.tmarkhotel.com/grand-myeongdong

3. Budget Hotels

a) Hotel Skypark Myeongdong III

Located in the heart of Myeongdong, Hotel Skypark Myeongdong III is a modern hotel that offers clean and comfortable rooms at an affordable price. The hotel's 120 rooms feature minimalist design with amenities such as flat-screen TVs, free Wi-Fi, and air conditioning.

The hotel's facilities include a 24-hour front desk, luggage storage, and a breakfast buffet. The hotel's location is perfect for exploring Myeongdong's shops, restaurants, and street food stalls, as well as nearby attractions like the Gyeongbokgung Palace and the Namsan Tower.

Average price: $50-$100 per night

Website: https://myeongdong3.skyparkhotel.com/

b) Hotel Aventree Jongno

Hotel Aventree Jongno is a stylish hotel located in the historic Jongno neighborhood. The hotel's 155 rooms feature modern design with amenities such as flat-screen TVs, minibars, and free Wi-Fi.

The hotel's facilities include a fitness center, a business center, and a breakfast buffet. The hotel's location is ideal for exploring Jongno's historic landmarks, such as the Gyeongbokgung Palace and the Changdeokgung Palace, as well as nearby attractions like the Insadong shopping district.

Average price: $50-$100 per night

Website: https://www.aventreehotel.com/jongno-eng

c) Starria Hostel Jongno

For budget-conscious travelers looking for a more unique experience, Starria Hostel Jongno offers affordable dorm-style and private rooms in the heart of the Jongno neighborhood. The hostel's rooms feature modern design with amenities such as free Wi-Fi and individual lockers.

The hostel's facilities include a common area with a kitchen, laundry facilities, and a rooftop terrace with stunning views of the city. The hostel's location is perfect for exploring Jongno's historic landmarks and attractions, as well as nearby neighborhoods like Insadong and Bukchon Hanok Village.

Average price: $20-$50 per night

Website: https://www.starriahostels.com/jongno

B. Guesthouses and Hostels

Guesthouses and hostels are a popular option for budget-conscious travelers who want to meet other travelers and experience local culture. Here are some recommendations:

a) K-Guesthouse Myeongdong 3

Located in the heart of Myeongdong, K-Guesthouse Myeongdong 3 is a cozy guesthouse that offers affordable and comfortable accommodations. The guesthouse's rooms feature modern design with amenities such as free Wi-Fi and air conditioning.

The guesthouse's facilities include a common area with a kitchen, a lounge, and a rooftop terrace with a panoramic view of the city. The guesthouse's location is perfect for exploring Myeongdong's shops, restaurants, and street food stalls, as well as nearby attractions like the Namsan Tower and the Gyeongbokgung Palace.

Average price: $30-$80 per night

Website: http://kguesthouse.co.kr/en/

b) Bunk Guesthouse Hongdae

Located in the trendy Hongdae neighborhood, Bunk Guesthouse is a modern and stylish hostel that offers dorm-style and private rooms. The hostel's rooms feature minimalist design with amenities such as free Wi-Fi and air conditioning.

The hostel's facilities include a common area with a kitchen, a lounge, and a rooftop terrace. The hostel's location is perfect for exploring Hongdae's vibrant nightlife, as well as nearby attractions like the Ewha Women's University and the Seoul World Cup Stadium.

Average price: $20-$50 per night

Website: https://www.bunkguesthouse.com/

Some more recommendations:

- Could you recommend some guesthouses or hostels that are in a great location for exploring the city?

Of course, here our top picks.

Hi Jun Guesthouse in Mapo-gu: https://booki.ng/2KeGjA7

Air Hostel Dongdaemun in Jongno-gu: https://booki.ng/2IxR8QD

K-Guesthouse in Jung-gu: https://booki.ng/2jUdFZW

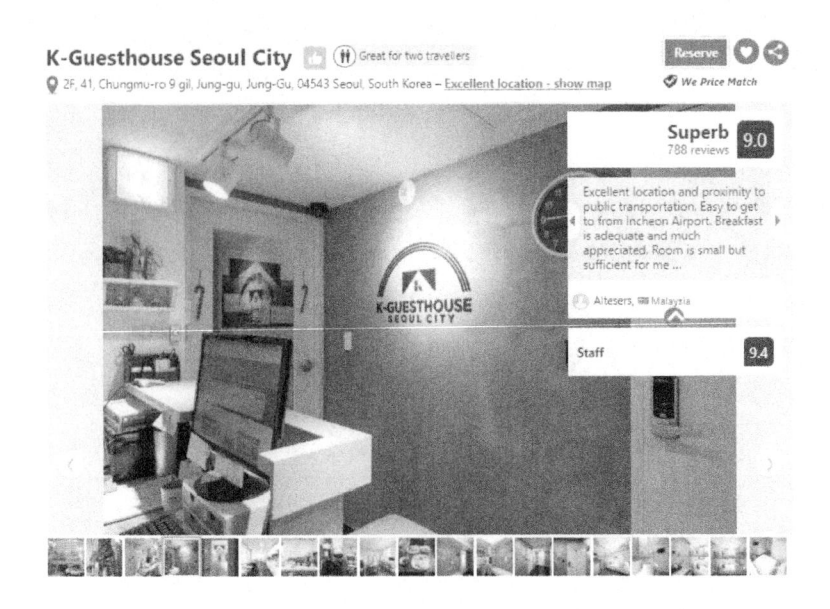

Seoul N Hostel in Jung-gu: https://booki.ng/2rCYmcg

C. Unique Stays

If you're looking for a more unique and immersive experience, Seoul offers several options for Hanok and Temple stays.

1. Hanok Stays

Hanoks are traditional Korean houses that feature a unique architectural style and design. Staying in a Hanok is a great way to experience traditional Korean culture and lifestyle. Here are some recommended Hanok stays:

a) Rakkojae Seoul

Rakkojae Seoul is a luxurious Hanok that offers traditional Korean-style rooms and suites. The Hanok's rooms feature antique furniture, traditional Korean bedding, and heated floors. The Hanok's facilities include a tea room, a garden, and a sauna.

The Hanok's location is perfect for exploring Bukchon Hanok Village, a historic neighborhood that features over 900 traditional Hanoks. The Hanok is also within walking distance of the Gyeongbokgung Palace and the Changdeokgung Palace.

Average price: $300-$500 per night

Website: https://rakkojae.com/seoul/

b) Doo Guesthouse

Doo Guesthouse is a charming Hanok that offers affordable and comfortable accommodations. The guesthouse's rooms feature traditional Korean-style design with modern amenities such as free Wi-Fi and air conditioning.

The guesthouse's facilities include a common area with a kitchen, a lounge, and a rooftop terrace with a panoramic view of the city. The guesthouse's location is perfect for exploring Bukchon Hanok Village and nearby attractions like the Gyeongbokgung Palace and the Insa-dong shopping district.

Average price: $50-$100 per night

Website: https://www.booking.com/hotel/kr/doo-guesthouse.en-gb.html

2. Temple Stays

Temple stays are a unique and immersive way to experience Korean Buddhism and temple life. Temple stays offer guests the opportunity to participate in Buddhist rituals, meditation, and communal meals.

Here are some recommended Temple Stays in Seoul:

a) Jogyesa Temple Stay

Jogyesa Temple is one of the most prominent Buddhist temples in Korea and is located in the heart of Seoul. The Temple Stay program at Jogyesa offers guests the opportunity to experience temple life and participate in Buddhist rituals, meditation, and chanting.

The program includes accommodations in traditional Korean-style rooms, communal meals, and guided tours of the temple grounds. Guests can also participate in cultural activities such as tea ceremonies and lantern-making workshops.

Average price: $70-$100 per night

Website: http://eng.templestay.com/

b) Bongeunsa Temple Stay

Bongeunsa Temple is a historic temple located in the Gangnam district of Seoul. The Temple Stay program at Bongeunsa offers guests the opportunity to experience temple life and participate in Buddhist rituals, meditation, and communal meals.

The program includes accommodations in traditional Korean-style rooms, guided tours of the temple grounds, and cultural activities such as tea ceremonies and meditation classes. Guests can also participate in the temple's volunteer program, which involves helping with temple chores and maintenance.

Average price: $70-$100 per night

Website: http://eng.templestay.com/

Temple Stays offer a unique and authentic way to experience Korean culture and Buddhism. They provide a peaceful and spiritual retreat from the hustle and bustle of the city, and guests can gain a deeper understanding of Korean traditions and way of life.

D. Our Recommended Budget Stay

Our favorite accommodation is **Bukchonmaru Hanok Guesthouse** that is run by a very friendly Korean family. It is located in the heart of Bukchon Hanok Village – the village that has the highest concentration of Korean traditional houses (*hanok*). The guesthouse has several family rooms with private bathroom (suitable for 2-6 people) and double rooms with shared bathroom. Traditional Korean breakfast is also included in a room rate, so you will be able to try handmade breakfast with lots of side dishes, rice, soup, and porridge. We have selected this guesthouse as accommodation for our three days itinerary as it is close to the main attractions of Seoul and lets you get to know Korean culture. However, you are welcome to stay in any other guesthouse, hotel or an apartment, and you will find a detailed guide to Seoul neighborhoods and accommodation down below.

Bukchonmaru Hanok Guesthouse with rating score from booking.com

Address: 2-164, Gye-dong, Jogno-gu; see on the map: http://bit.ly/2I6RZbE

Book: http://www.bukchonmaru.com/en/reservation/; https://booki.ng/2rCcnWM

Price per night: Double room 90 000 won ($90) or 110 000 won ($110, 2 people); Family room 140 000 won ($140, 2 people) + 20 000 won ($20) for every additional person. **Tip!:** find better deals on various websites like booking.com.

Recommended: Traditional Korean stay and food, great views, close to major city's attractions and great restaurants and located in the historic neighborhood.

E. Frequently Asked Questions about Staying in Seoul

Q: Where to stay in Seoul if I am traveling on a budget?

If you are looking for budget-friendly accommodation in Seoul, there are several options to choose from. You can select to stay in cheap accommodation or stay close to the main tourist attractions and spend less money on transportation. Areas around universities are pretty cheap as you can find various hostels and guesthouses such as Hyehwa, Cheongpa-dong, Sinchon or Heukseok-dong. These neighborhoods aren't too far from major tourist destinations either.

Q: Can I rent an Airbnb?

Yes, renting an Airbnb is an option in Seoul. However, it is essential to research the area and choose wisely. It is recommended to rent an apartment instead of a private room as private rooms can be more expensive than a nice guesthouse. Make sure you check the location and the proximity of the subway station to your accommodation. You don't want to stay in a remote area with no easy access to transportation.

Q: Which subway line is the most convenient?

Seoul has more than 20 subway lines, and all of them are convenient for certain areas and transferring. While looking for accommodation, you should check the closest subway station, line, its stops, and transfer points. We recommend staying close to subway lines nr. 1 or nr. 4 as they are the main lines of Seoul. If your selected accommodation doesn't have those subway lines, make sure that there are at least two different subway lines close to your accommodation so you will have a choice. This way, you can travel to different parts of the city quickly and efficiently.

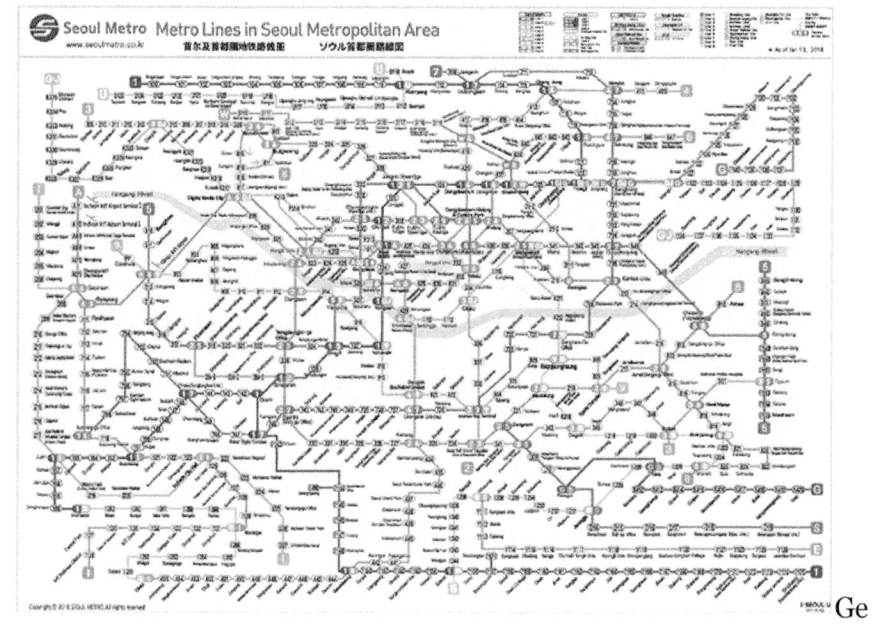

Get the full-sized map here: *http://bit.ly/2KTXMPe*

Very useful guide about Seoul subway: https://english.visitkorea.or.kr:1001/enu/TRP/TP_ENG_6.jsp

Q: Where can I stay in Seoul if I want to go shopping?

A: Seoul has several popular shopping areas. For cheap and fashionable clothes, Hongdae (Hongik University) or Ehwa Women's University Fashion Street are the most famous. Staying in these areas can also be budget-friendly, with plenty of affordable guesthouses and hostels to choose from. Myeong-dong is another famous shopping street, filled with makeup stores, clothing boutiques, and souvenir shops. The Gangnam Express Bus Terminal underground shopping mall is also a great option for affordable clothing. However, staying in Gangnam can be more expensive than other areas in Seoul.

Q: Do hotels, guesthouses, and hostels offer special tours for discounted prices?

A: Yes, many hotels, guesthouses, and hostels offer special tours for discounted prices. Some even provide free walking tours of Seoul or discounted tickets for the Seoul sightseeing bus. Check the website of your preferred accommodation before booking to see if they offer any special deals or packages.

Q: Is it good to have breakfast included in my room rate?

A: Yes, most accommodations in Seoul offer breakfast included in the room rate. This can be a great option, as many hotels and guesthouses provide a continental buffet with plenty of options to choose from. Some traditional guesthouses may even offer a full Korean breakfast, which can be a unique and filling experience. Having breakfast included in your room rate can also save you time and money, as you won't have to wake up early to search for food in an unfamiliar city.

IV. Sightseeing

A. Historical Sites

Seoul is a city steeped in history, and there are many historical sites to explore. Here are some of the top historical sites to visit in Seoul:

1. Gyeongbokgung Palace

Gyeongbokgung Palace is the largest and most iconic palace in Seoul. Built in 1395, it was the main palace of the Joseon Dynasty and served as the seat of power for over 500 years. The palace was heavily damaged during the Japanese invasion in the late 16th century, but extensive restoration efforts have restored it to its former glory.

Visitors to Gyeongbokgung Palace can explore its grand halls, pavilions, and gardens. The Changing of the Guard ceremony takes place every hour from 10 a.m. to 3 p.m. and is a popular attraction.

Entrance fee: 3,000 won ($2.60)

Website: http://www.royalpalace.go.kr/

2. Changdeokgung Palace

Changdeokgung Palace is another major palace in Seoul and was the second seat of power during the Joseon Dynasty. It was built in the early 15th century and has been designated as a UNESCO World Heritage Site.

The palace features beautiful gardens, including the famous Huwon Secret Garden, which is a serene and peaceful retreat from the busy city. Guided tours are available in English and other languages.

Entrance fee: 3,000 won ($2.60)

Website: http://www.changdeokgung.go.kr/

3. Deoksugung Palace

Deoksugung Palace is a smaller palace located in the heart of Seoul's business district. It was built in the late 16th century and served as the residence of various Joseon Dynasty kings.

The palace's main attraction is the Changing of the Guard ceremony, which takes place three times a day. Visitors can also explore the palace's various halls and pavilions.

Entrance fee: 1,000 won ($0.87)

Website: http://www.deoksugung.go.kr/

4. Jongmyo Shrine

Jongmyo Shrine is a UNESCO World Heritage Site and was the ancestral shrine of the Joseon Dynasty. It was built in the late 14th century and served as the site for ancestral rites and ceremonies.

Visitors can take a guided tour of the shrine and learn about the history and significance of the site. The shrine is surrounded by a beautiful forested park and is a peaceful retreat from the bustling city.

Entrance fee: 1,000 won ($0.87)

Website: http://jm.cha.go.kr/

B. Modern Attractions

Seoul is not only a city with a rich history but also a modern metropolis with many modern attractions to explore. Here are some of the top modern attractions in Seoul:

1. N Seoul Tower

N Seoul Tower is a 237-meter-tall tower located on top of Namsan Mountain. It was built in 1969 as a telecommunications tower and has since become one of the most iconic landmarks in Seoul.

Visitors can take a cable car or hike up to the tower and enjoy panoramic views of the city. There are also restaurants, cafes, and gift shops inside the tower.

Entrance fee: 10,000 won ($8.70)

Website: https://www.nseoultower.com/

2. Lotte World Tower

Lotte World Tower is a 555-meter-tall skyscraper located in the Jamsil district of Seoul. It is the tallest building in Korea and the fifth tallest in the world.

Visitors can take an elevator to the observation deck on the 118th floor and enjoy stunning views of the city. The tower also features a luxury hotel, shopping mall, and aquarium.

Entrance fee: 27,000 won ($23.50)

Website: https://www.lwt.co.kr/en/

3. Dongdaemun Design Plaza

Dongdaemun Design Plaza is a futuristic building located in the Dongdaemun fashion district of Seoul. It was designed by renowned architect Zaha Hadid and opened in 2014.

The building features exhibition spaces, a design museum, and a conference center. Visitors can also explore the nearby Dongdaemun Market, which is one of the largest and oldest markets in Korea.

Entrance fee: Varies by exhibition

Website: http://www.ddp.or.kr/

C. Parks and Nature

Seoul is not only a bustling city but also has plenty of parks and natural attractions to explore. Here are some of the top parks and nature spots in Seoul:

1. Namsan Park

Namsan Park is a 262-meter-tall mountain located in the heart of Seoul. It is a popular park for hiking and offers stunning views of the city.

The park also features the Namsan Tower, a traditional Korean village, and a botanical garden. Visitors can hike or take a cable car to the top of the mountain.

Entrance fee: Free, but there is a fee for the cable car

Website: http://english.visitseoul.net/attractions/Namsan-Park_/19

2. Hangang River Park

Hangang River Park is a series of parks along the Hangang River that flows through Seoul. It is a popular spot for picnics, bike rides, and water activities.

The park features numerous attractions such as playgrounds, gardens, and sports facilities. Visitors can also take a river cruise to enjoy the scenic views of the city from the water.

Entrance fee: Free

Website: https://english.visitkorea.or.kr/enu/ATR/SI_EN_3_1_1_1.jsp?cid=264308

3. Bukhansan National Park

Bukhansan National Park is a mountainous park located in northern Seoul. It is a popular spot for hiking and offers stunning views of the city and surrounding mountains.

The park features numerous hiking trails, temples, and historical sites. Visitors can also take a cable car to the top of the mountain for panoramic views of the city.

Entrance fee: Free

Website: http://english.knps.or.kr/Knp/Bukhansan/

D. Museums and Cultural Centers

Seoul is home to a wide range of museums and cultural centers that offer a fascinating insight into Korea's rich history, art, and culture. Here are some must-visit museums and cultural centers in Seoul:

1. National Museum of Korea

The National Museum of Korea is the largest museum in Korea and houses over 220,000 artifacts, including relics from the prehistoric era to the modern age. The museum's vast collection includes ceramics, sculptures, paintings, calligraphy, and more. The museum's permanent exhibition is divided into three main galleries: Prehistory and Ancient History, Medieval and Early Modern History, and Modern and Contemporary History. The museum also features special exhibitions, educational programs, and cultural events throughout the year.

Address: 137 Seobinggo-ro, Yongsan-gu, Seoul Hours: 10:00am - 6:00pm (Closed on Mondays) Admission: Free

2. **War Memorial of Korea**

The War Memorial of Korea is a museum and memorial dedicated to the country's military history and the Korean War. The museum's exhibits include a range of military artifacts, weapons, uniforms, and vehicles. Visitors can learn about the history of the Korean War and its impact on Korean society, as well as pay tribute to the sacrifices made by Korean soldiers and their allies.

Address: 29, Itaewon-ro, Yongsan-gu, Seoul Hours: 9:00am - 6:00pm (Closed on Mondays) Admission: Free

3. **Leeum Samsung Museum of Art**

The Leeum Samsung Museum of Art is a contemporary art museum that houses a collection of traditional Korean art and modern and contemporary art from Korea and around the world. The museum's collection includes paintings, sculptures, installations, and video art. The museum is divided into three sections: Samsung Museum of Art, Leeum Gallery, and Plateau, each with its unique focus and atmosphere.

Address: 60-16 Itaewon-ro 55-gil, Hannam-dong, Yongsan-gu, Seoul Hours: 10:30am - 6:00pm (Closed on Mondays) Admission: 10,000 won for adults, 6,000 won for students and seniors

Other notable museums and cultural centers in Seoul include the Seoul Museum of Art, the Korean Folk Village, the Seoul Arts Center, and the Namsangol Hanok Village. With so many museums and cultural centers to choose from, visitors to Seoul can immerse themselves in Korean culture and history, and experience the best that the city has to offer.

E. Off-the-Beaten-Path Attractions

Seoul is a city full of surprises, with many hidden gems waiting to be discovered. If you're looking for something off the beaten path, here are some unique attractions that are worth checking out:

Ihwa Mural Village

Located in the heart of Seoul, the Ihwa Mural Village is a vibrant neighborhood known for its colorful murals and street art. The neighborhood was once a rundown area, but it has been transformed into an art hub with the help of local artists and community members. Visitors can explore the winding alleys and staircases while taking in the stunning artwork.

Seoul Forest

Escape the hustle and bustle of the city by visiting Seoul Forest, a vast green space that spans over 1.1 million square meters. The park features walking trails, picnic areas, and a variety of flora and fauna. There are also several cultural and art installations throughout the park, including the Seoul Forest Art Center and the Forest of Wisdom.

Seodaemun Prison History Hall

History buffs will appreciate a visit to the Seodaemun Prison History Hall, a former prison that played a significant role in Korea's struggle for independence from Japan. The museum features exhibits and artifacts that tell the stories of the prisoners who were held there during the Japanese occupation.

Bukchon Hanok Village

Bukchon Hanok Village is a charming neighborhood that has preserved the traditional Korean-style houses called hanoks. Visitors can wander the narrow alleys and admire the beautiful architecture while learning about traditional Korean culture. There are also several cafes and galleries throughout the village that offer a glimpse into modern Korean culture.

Seonyudo Park

Seonyudo Park is a small island located in the Han River that has been transformed into an urban oasis. The park features lush greenery, walking trails, and a unique water treatment facility that has been turned into an art installation. Visitors can also take in the stunning views of the city skyline from the park's observatory.

These off-the-beaten-path attractions offer a unique perspective on Seoul and are perfect for travelers looking to explore beyond the typical tourist hotspots.

V. Shopping

A. Shopping Districts

Seoul is a paradise for shoppers, offering a variety of shopping districts catering to different styles, preferences, and budgets. Here are some of the top shopping districts in Seoul:

Myeongdong

Located in the heart of Seoul, Myeongdong is one of the most popular shopping districts in the city. This bustling area is known for its trendy fashion boutiques, cosmetic shops, and street food stalls. Here you can find a range of popular Korean beauty brands like Innisfree, Etude House, and Missha. It's also home to several department stores, including Lotte Department Store and Shinsegae Department Store.

Insadong

For a more traditional shopping experience, head to Insadong. This historic district is famous for its antique shops, art galleries, and traditional Korean craft shops. You can find unique souvenirs and traditional Korean items like hanbok (Korean traditional clothing), pottery, and calligraphy supplies. It's also an excellent place to experience Korean tea culture, with several teahouses and cafes offering traditional Korean teas and snacks.

Gangnam

Gangnam is known as one of the wealthiest and trendiest districts in Seoul, offering high-end shopping and entertainment options. The main shopping areas in Gangnam are Apgujeong and Garosu-gil. Apgujeong is home to luxury fashion boutiques and designer shops, while Garosu-gil offers a more laid-back shopping experience with trendy fashion and lifestyle boutiques.

B. Markets

In addition to shopping districts, Seoul is also home to several vibrant markets offering a wide range of products and experiences. Here are some of the top markets to visit in Seoul:

Namdaemun Market

Namdaemun Market is one of the oldest and largest traditional markets in Seoul, with over 10,000 shops selling everything from clothing and accessories to food and souvenirs. It's a great place to find traditional Korean items like ginseng, hanbok, and traditional snacks like hotteok (sweet pancakes) and tteokbokki (spicy rice cakes).

Gwangjang Market

Gwangjang Market is a bustling food market that's been around since 1905. It's a great place to sample traditional Korean street food like bindaetteok (mung bean pancakes), tteokbokki, and bibimbap (mixed rice with vegetables and meat). You can also find a range of textiles, clothing, and handicrafts at the market.

Dongdaemun Market

Dongdaemun Market is a massive shopping complex that's open 24 hours a day. It's a great place to shop for clothing, accessories, and textiles, with over 26 shopping malls and thousands of shops. You can also find several food stalls and restaurants offering Korean and international cuisine. The market is particularly popular for its wholesale fashion options, making it a great place to shop for business or personal needs.

C. Malls and Department Stores

Seoul is known for its modern and sophisticated shopping centers, which offer a wide range of options for shoppers. Here are some of the top malls and department stores in Seoul:

Lotte Department Store

Lotte Department Store is a popular upscale shopping destination in Seoul, with several locations throughout the city, including the main store in Myeong-dong. The store offers a wide range of luxury brands, cosmetics, electronics, and home goods. Lotte Department Store also has a food court, grocery store, and duty-free shopping for international visitors. The Myeong-dong store is open from 10 am to 8 pm daily and is located at 81 Namdaemun-ro, Jung-gu, Seoul.

Website: https://www.lotteshopping.com/

COEX Mall

COEX Mall is one of the largest underground shopping centers in Asia, located in the Gangnam district of Seoul. The mall offers a vast selection of shops, ranging from high-end boutiques to affordable fashion brands, along with restaurants, a movie theater, and an aquarium. COEX Mall is open from 10:30 am to 8 pm daily and is located at 513 Yeongdong-daero, Samseong 1(il)-dong, Gangnam-gu, Seoul.

Website: https://www.coexmall.com/eng/index.jsp

IFC Mall

IFC Mall is a luxury shopping center located in the Yeouido district of Seoul. The mall features high-end brands such as Prada, Louis Vuitton, and Gucci, along with a selection of restaurants, cafes, and a cinema. IFC Mall also has a rooftop garden with views of the Han River. The mall is open from 10:30 am to 8 pm daily and is located at 10 Gukjegeumyung-ro, Yeongdeungpo-gu, Seoul.

Website: https://ifcmallseoul.com/

Doota Mall

Doota Mall is a popular shopping center in the Dongdaemun area of Seoul, known for its affordable fashion brands and trendy streetwear. The mall features several floors of shops, a food court, and a rooftop garden. Doota Mall is open from 10:30 am to 5 am daily and is located at 275 Jangchungdan-ro, Euljiro 6(yuk)-ga, Jung-gu, Seoul.

Website: https://www.dootamall.co.kr/en/

Shinsegae Centum City

Shinsegae Centum City is a massive shopping complex located in Busan, but it's worth the trip from Seoul for its sheer size and luxury offerings. With a Guinness World Record as the largest department store in the world, this shopping mecca boasts numerous floors of high-end fashion and beauty brands, a spa, a golf range, and even an ice rink. The mall is open from 10:30 am to 8 pm daily and is located at 1495 U-dong, Haeundae-gu, Busan.

Website: https://www.shinsegae.com/eng/main/index.jsp

D. Specialty Shops and Souvenirs

Seoul is famous for its unique and quirky specialty shops and souvenirs. Here are some of the best places to find them:

Gyeongdong Market - This traditional market is famous for its medicinal herbs and traditional Korean medicines. It's a great place to find unique souvenirs, including herbal teas, soaps, and beauty products. The market is open from 9 am to 6 pm daily and is located at 102, Jegi-ro, Dongdaemun-gu, Seoul.

Insa-dong - This quaint neighborhood is known for its traditional Korean arts and crafts. It's a great place to find unique souvenirs, such as traditional Korean pottery, paper lanterns, and handmade jewelry. Insa-dong is open from 10 am to 10 pm daily and is located at 62, Insadong-gil, Jongno-gu, Seoul.

Namsangol Hanok Village - This traditional Korean village is a great place to shop for handmade Korean crafts and souvenirs. The village has several shops that sell traditional Korean clothing, pottery, and accessories. The village is open from 9 am to 9 pm daily and is located at 28, Toegye-ro 34-gil, Pil-dong, Jung-gu, Seoul.

Tongin Market - This traditional market is famous for its street food and Korean snacks. It's a great place to find unique snacks and souvenirs, such as Korean rice cakes, traditional candies, and dried fish. The market is open from 11 am to 4 pm daily and is located at 18, Jahamun-ro 15-gil, Jongno-gu, Seoul.

Dongdaemun Market - This massive market is famous for its fashion and clothing. It's a great place to find unique clothing, accessories, and souvenirs at affordable prices. The market is open 24 hours a day and is located at 265, Dongho-ro, Jung-gu, Seoul.

E. Tips for Shopping in Seoul

If you're planning to do some shopping in Seoul, here are some tips to help you make the most of your experience:

1. Bring cash and credit cards: While credit cards are widely accepted in Seoul, some smaller shops and markets may only accept cash. Make sure to bring both just in case.

2. Bargaining is not common: Unlike in some other Asian countries, bargaining is not a common practice in South Korea.

Prices are usually fixed, so don't be surprised if the price is not negotiable.

3. Check for tax refunds: If you spend over a certain amount at certain stores, you may be eligible for a tax refund. Make sure to ask the store for a tax refund form and keep all receipts.

4. Try before you buy: Many shops offer testers or samples for you to try before making a purchase. Take advantage of these opportunities to ensure you're happy with your purchase.

5. Look for deals and discounts: Seoul is known for its sales and discounts, so keep an eye out for signs and advertisements. Many shops also offer loyalty programs and discounts for members.

6. Don't forget about customs regulations: If you plan on buying souvenirs like traditional Korean pottery or ginseng, make sure to check the customs regulations in your home country to avoid any issues at the airport.

7. Keep an eye on the time: Some shops and markets close early or have limited hours on certain days of the week, so make sure to check their hours before heading out.

VI. Food and Dining

A. Traditional Korean Cuisine

Korean cuisine is known for its bold flavors, fresh ingredients, and healthy options. From savory meat dishes to spicy vegetarian fare, there is something for everyone in Seoul's food scene.

One of the most popular traditional Korean dishes is **kimchi**, a fermented vegetable dish made with cabbage, radish, or cucumber. It's served as a side dish with nearly every meal and is believed to have numerous health benefits. Another must-try dish is bibimbap, a bowl of rice topped with vegetables, meat or tofu, and a fried egg. It's often served with a side of spicy chili paste for added flavor.

If you're feeling adventurous, try some Korean street food like **tteokbokki**, a spicy rice cake dish, or **hotteok**, a sweet pancake filled with cinnamon and brown sugar. For meat lovers, Korean BBQ is a must-try. Restaurants often have grills at each table where you can cook your own meat, such as bulgogi (marinated beef) or galbi (short ribs).

For those with dietary restrictions, vegetarian and vegan options are also available. Many traditional Korean dishes can be made without meat or substituted with **tofu.**

Some popular traditional Korean restaurants in Seoul include **Jungsik,** which offers modern interpretations of classic Korean dishes, and **Gwangjang Market,** a bustling food market with a wide variety of street food and traditional Korean dishes.

Here are more details about the dishes:

Kimchi

Kimchi is pickled spicy cabbage that is usually served as a side dish with main dishes. You can eat it with anything you order and every restaurant has its own recipe of kimchi, so it never tastes the same.

Samgyeopsal

Samgyeopsal is a pork belly that is usually eaten during bbq at the restaurant. You have to grill by yourself and wrap it in the lettuce together with various side dishes, kimchi, rice and salty sauce that comes with it. It is priced per 100g, so can be quite pricey as 100g is usually 10 000 won ($10). However, it comes with lots of side dishes and stews, so the price pays off.

Bulgogi

Bulgogi is marinated beef/pork strips with lots of sesame oil, garlic and soy sauce, and grilled. Usually served over rice, but can be

served over noodles or combined into the dish such as Japchae, Kimbap, and Bibimbap. Prices vary, pork bulgogi is usually 8000 won ($8) per plate, and beef bulgogi can be from 8000 won to 10 000 won ($8-$10) depending on a restaurant and area you are eating.

Kimchi Stew

Very affordable and filling dish. Kimchi stew is made of kimchi, pork chunks, potatoes, and few other vegetables. Usually is a very spicy dish that is served boiling hot in a traditional Korean stoneware. The price is about 5000 won ($5).

Seolleongtang

Seolleongtang is a Korean ox bone soup that broth and meat were simmered for long hours on low heat. It is a very traditional Korean soup and compared to other dishes is very plain as you can add yourself what you prefer such as salt, chilies and etc. It's usually served in stoneware with some noodles and few side dishes. Price is about 6000 won ($6).

Dolsot Bibimbap

Dolsot Bibimbap is a very common Korean dish that is made from rice mixed with/without meat, egg, various vegetables, and sesame oil and chili paste. It's not a spicy dish as you can add chili paste by yourself. It's served to boil hot in a traditional stoneware with various side dishes. Price can be from 4000 won to 6500 won ($4-$6.5) depending on a restaurant and area.

Mandu

Mandu is a Korean dumplings that are steamed and made from thin rice dough and filled with sweet potato noodles, vegetables, and meat. You can get a prawn mandu and vegetarian mandu. Also, you will be able to find them at small restaurants and street food vendors. Price is 3000 won ($3) per 6 or 10 mandu depending on the restaurant.

Naengmyeon

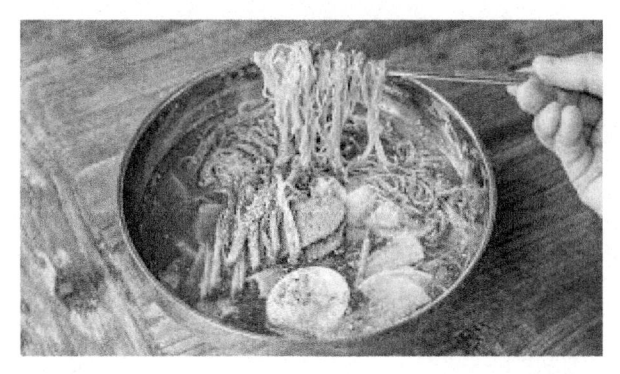

Naengmyeon literally translates as ice noodles and it actually is. Buckwheat noodles are boiled and served in an iced broth with some sliced vegetables, boiled egg and sometimes meat. This dish is very popular during the summer. Price: 3000 won to 5000 won ($3-$5).

Kimbap

Kimbap is very similar to sushi but instead of fish, there is ham with various vegetables and sliced omelet. There are restaurants that serve different kinds of kimbap. This seaweed roll is very popular as a snack food that can be packed for hiking, picnic or a long walk. Price: 1500 won ($1.50) per roll. However, if you want a fancier kimbap such as tuna mayo or prawn, you will pay more.

B. Street Food

Seoul is known for its diverse and delicious street food scene, where you can find a variety of dishes at affordable prices. Here are some of the must-try street foods in Seoul:

1. Tteokbokki - Spicy rice cakes served in a thick, red sauce made with gochujang (red pepper paste).
2. Japchae - Stir-fried glass noodles mixed with vegetables and beef or pork.
3. Hotteok - A sweet and chewy pancake filled with brown sugar, cinnamon, and chopped nuts.
4. Kimbap - A Korean version of sushi, made with rice, seaweed, and various fillings such as vegetables, meat, or egg.
5. Fried Chicken - Korean fried chicken is crispy on the outside and juicy on the inside, served with various dipping sauces.
6. Bungeoppang - Fish-shaped pastries filled with sweet red bean paste or custard.
7. Mandu - Korean-style dumplings filled with meat and vegetables.
8. Odeng - Fish cakes served in a hot and savory broth.
9. Gyeran-bbang - Egg bread, a popular Korean street food made with a fluffy and sweet bread filled with a whole egg.
10. Twigim - Deep-fried vegetables, seafood, or meat served on a skewer.

To find the best street food in Seoul, head to popular areas such as Myeong-dong, Namdaemun Market, Gwangjang Market, and Dongdaemun Market. Make sure to have cash on hand, as most street vendors do not accept credit cards.

While street food in Seoul is generally safe to eat, it's always a good idea to look for vendors with a high turnover of customers and to avoid raw or undercooked foods. If you have any food allergies, make sure to communicate this clearly with the vendor before ordering.

C. Themed Cafes and Unique Dining Experiences

Seoul is known for its vibrant and unique themed cafes and dining experiences. Here are some recommendations for those looking for an unforgettable culinary experience in Seoul:

1. Thanks Nature Cafe - This cozy cafe in Hongdae is home to two resident sheep that roam around the outdoor patio area. Patrons can enjoy delicious coffee and waffles while petting and interacting with the sheep.

Address: 486, Seogyo-dong, Mapo-gu, Seoul Hours: Daily 11am-9pm Website: https://www.instagram.com/thanks.naturecafe/?hl=en

2. Blind Alley - This cat cafe in the Gangnam area is the perfect spot for cat lovers. Guests can enjoy coffee and snacks while playing with the resident cats.

Address: 50, Gangnam-daero 102-gil, Gangnam-gu, Seoul Hours: Daily 12pm-10pm Website: https://www.instagram.com/blindalley_cat/?hl=en

3. Monster Cupcakes - This bakery in Hongdae specializes in unique and creative cupcakes with monster-inspired designs. Their signature "Monster Cupcake" is a must-try for anyone with a sweet tooth.

Address: 394-35 Seogyo-dong, Mapo-gu, Seoul Hours: Daily 11am-10pm Website: https://www.instagram.com/monster_cupcakes/?hl=en

4. Gwangjang Market - This historic market in central Seoul offers a wide variety of traditional Korean street food and snacks, including bindaetteok (mung bean pancakes), tteokbokki (spicy rice cakes), and kimbap (Korean sushi rolls).

Address: 88, Changgyeonggung-ro, Jongno-gu, Seoul Hours: Daily 8:30am-11pm Website: https://www.visitseoul.net/en/article/article.do?_method=view&m=0004007002012&p=07&art_id=37967&lang=en

5. Poop Cafe - This quirky cafe in Insadong serves drinks and desserts shaped like poop. The unique theme and decor make for a memorable and Instagram-worthy experience.

Address: 102-10 Gwanhun-dong, Jongno-gu, Seoul Hours: Daily 10:30am-9pm Website: https://www.instagram.com/poopcafe_/?hl=en

6. BBQ Olive Chicken - This popular Korean fried chicken chain offers a variety of unique and delicious flavors, such as honey mustard and garlic soy sauce. Perfect for a casual and satisfying dining experience.

Address: Multiple locations throughout Seoul Hours: Varies by location Website: https://www.bbq.co.kr/en/index.asp

Whether you're looking for a cute and cuddly cafe experience or a unique twist on traditional Korean cuisine, Seoul offers plenty of options to satisfy any foodie's cravings.

D. International Cuisine

Seoul is a vibrant and diverse city, and this is reflected in its international cuisine scene. Visitors can find a wide range of international foods from all over the world, from Japanese sushi to Italian pizza, Mexican tacos to Indian curry. Here are some of the best international cuisine options in Seoul:

1. Itaewon - Itaewon is the go-to place in Seoul for international cuisine, with a variety of restaurants serving dishes from all around the world. There are many options for Western food, including burgers, pizza, and steak. The area also has a large Muslim community, and there are several halal restaurants serving Middle Eastern and South Asian food. Some popular restaurants in Itaewon include Vatos Urban Tacos, Namsan Chemistry, and Gobble & Guzzle.

2. Garosu-gil - Garosu-gil is a trendy and fashionable street in Gangnam, known for its cafes, boutiques, and upscale restaurants. It is also home to a variety of international cuisine options, including Italian, French, and Japanese. Some popular restaurants in Garosu-gil include Tartine, La Tavola, and Plant.

3. Hannam-dong - Hannam-dong is a quiet residential area near Itaewon, and it has several excellent international cuisine options. The area is particularly known for its French restaurants, including L'Impasse and Pierre Gagnaire. Hannam-

dong is also home to several Japanese restaurants, including Sushi Cho and Yakiniku Jumbo Hanare.

4. Hongdae - Hongdae is a lively neighborhood known for its arts and culture scene, and it also has several international cuisine options. The area has a large number of restaurants serving Japanese food, including sushi and ramen. There are also several Mexican restaurants, including Gusto Taco and On the Border. Hongdae also has several fusion restaurants that blend Korean and Western cuisine, such as Morococo Cafe and Tuk Tuk Noodle Thai.

5. Jamsil - Jamsil is a neighborhood in southern Seoul known for its amusement parks, sports facilities, and shopping centers. It is also home to several excellent international cuisine options. Some popular restaurants in Jamsil include Italian restaurant Cima, Japanese restaurant Yurim, and Vietnamese restaurant Banh Mi.

E. Vegetarian and Vegan Options

Seoul has a growing number of vegetarian and vegan restaurants, making it easier for plant-based eaters to find delicious food options. Here are some places to check out:

1. Plant

Plant is a vegan restaurant that serves up a variety of healthy dishes made with organic ingredients. The menu includes burgers, salads, bowls, and smoothies. They also offer raw desserts and a selection of organic wines and beers.

Address: 2F, 74, Wausan-ro 29-gil, Mapo-gu, Seoul Website: https://www.instagram.com/plant.fooddrink/

2. Ose Gye Hyang

Ose Gye Hyang is a vegan restaurant that specializes in traditional Korean cuisine. They offer a range of dishes made with tofu, mushrooms, and other plant-based ingredients. The menu includes soups, stews, and rice dishes, and they also offer a set menu for two people.

Address: 36-15, Samcheong-ro 4-gil, Jongno-gu, Seoul Website: https://www.facebook.com/osegyehyang/

3. The Bread Blue

The Bread Blue is a vegan bakery that offers a wide selection of bread, cakes, and pastries made with organic and natural ingredients. They have a cozy atmosphere and also offer coffee and tea.

Address: 76, Bukchon-ro 11-gil, Jongno-gu, Seoul Website: https://www.instagram.com/thebreadblue/

4. Plant Cafe

Plant Cafe is a vegan cafe that serves a variety of plant-based dishes, including salads, sandwiches, and smoothie bowls. They also offer coffee and tea.

Address: 76-1, Itaewon-ro 27ga-gil, Yongsan-gu, Seoul Website: https://www.instagram.com/plantcafeseoul/

5. Balwoo Gongyang

Balwoo Gongyang is a Michelin-starred vegetarian restaurant that serves traditional Korean temple cuisine. The menu changes seasonally and features dishes made with locally-sourced, organic ingredients. They also offer a templestay program that includes a temple tour and a temple food cooking class.

Address: 56, Ujeongguk-ro, Jongno-gu, Seoul Website: https://www.balwoo.or.kr/eng/temple_cuisine/intro_temple_cuisine.do

F. Tips for Dining in Seoul

Seoul is a foodie paradise, with a vast range of dining options to suit every taste and budget. Here are some tips to help make your dining experience in Seoul more enjoyable:

1. Learn some basic Korean phrases: Even if you don't speak Korean fluently, learning a few key phrases can go a long way in making your dining experience more comfortable. For example, "hello" is "annyeonghaseyo," "thank you" is "gamsahamnida," and "please" is "ju-se-yo."

2. Try street food: Seoul's street food scene is famous for its delicious and unique offerings. Try local favorites like tteokbokki (spicy rice cakes), hotteok (sweet pancakes filled with cinnamon and sugar), and mandu (dumplings).

3. Check for English menus: Many restaurants in Seoul have English menus or pictures of their dishes to help non-Korean speakers navigate their options. If you're not sure, don't be afraid to ask for help or use translation apps.

4. Consider vegetarian or vegan options: While traditional Korean cuisine often includes meat and fish, there are plenty of vegetarian and vegan options available in Seoul. Look for dishes like bibimbap (mixed rice bowl with vegetables), japchae (stir-fried glass noodles with vegetables), or kimbap (Korean sushi rolls).

5. Make reservations: Popular restaurants in Seoul can get crowded, especially during peak dining hours. Consider making a reservation in advance to ensure a spot.

6. Take off your shoes: Many traditional Korean restaurants require guests to take off their shoes before entering. Look for a shoe rack near the entrance or ask the staff for guidance.

7. Mind your chopsticks: In Korea, it's considered rude to point with chopsticks, spear food with them, or leave them standing upright in a bowl of rice. Instead, use chopsticks to pick up food and use the spoon provided for soups and stews.

8. Don't rush: In Korean culture, meals are often seen as a social and communal activity, and it's not uncommon for a meal to last a few hours. Don't be in a rush to finish your meal and take the time to enjoy your dining experience.

G. Mini Guide to Coffee Shops in Seoul

- Billy Angel Cake Company

Has a few branches, very light atmosphere, perfect for photos and relax. Famous not only for the coffee but also for its cakes. More information: http://english.visitseoul.net/eat/Billy-Angel-Cake-Company-Gangnam-Station-Branch_/24178

- Dore Dore

French dessert and brunch café that can be found in a busy stylish street of Gangnam. Famous for its 100% house-roasted coffee and rainbow cake. More information and prices range is here: https://www.trazy.com/spot/2673/dore-dore-cafe-%EB%8F%84%EB%A0%88%EB%8F%84%EB%A0%88-%EC%B9%B4%ED%8E%98-restaurant-cafe

- Stylenanda Pink Pool Café

If you like pink, it will be your paradise. This coffee shop is very stylish and colorful, the perfect spot for social media photos. More information about the coffee shop: https://www.timeout.com/seoul/restaurants/stylenanda-pink-pool-cafe

- Suyeonsanbang

A completely different coffee shop from previously mentioned ones. Suyeonsanbang is a traditional hanok tea/coffee house that serves all kinds of traditional Korean tea and various desserts. It is a very famous spot between locals and foreigners. More information: http://english.visitkorea.or.kr/enu/ATR/SI_EN_3_1_1_1.jsp?cid=1721080

- Hello Kitty Café

Very pink and girly café popular between social media users as its design is perfect for photos. You can try various desserts and sweet drinks. Café website: http://www.hellokittycafe.co.kr/en/

- Insadong Chatjip

This teahouse serves homemade Korean traditional tea and is perfect hideaway from always noisy streets of Insadong. Traditional Korean music always plays in the teahouse and makes the atmosphere peaceful and relaxing. If you visit this tea house, make sure to try a Korean traditional shaved ice cream with your tea. Information about the teahouse:
http://english.visitkorea.or.kr/enu/ATR/SI_EN_3_1_1_1.jsp?cid=1065462

VII. Nightlife

A. Neighborhoods for Nightlife

Seoul has a vibrant and exciting nightlife scene, with many neighborhoods offering unique and diverse experiences. Here are three popular areas to explore for nightlife in Seoul:

Itaewon

Itaewon is one of the most multicultural neighborhoods in Seoul and is known for its diverse and lively nightlife. The area has a large concentration of international restaurants, bars, and nightclubs. Itaewon is popular with expats, tourists, and locals alike and offers a range of entertainment options, including live music, DJ sets, and karaoke bars.

Hongdae

Hongdae is a trendy and youthful neighborhood, popular with college students and young professionals. The area is known for its vibrant street performances, live music, and indie clubs. Hongdae offers a range of nightlife options, from small intimate bars to larger dance clubs, making it a great place to explore for those looking for a unique and exciting experience.

Gangnam

Gangnam is known for its luxury and upscale nightlife scene, with high-end clubs, lounges, and rooftop bars. The area is popular with trendy young professionals and is home to many popular K-pop celebrities. While the prices in Gangnam may be higher compared to other neighborhoods, it offers a luxurious and glamorous atmosphere for those looking for a high-end nightlife experience.

B. Bars and Clubs

Seoul has a vibrant nightlife scene with numerous bars and clubs catering to a range of tastes and preferences. Here are some popular options to check out:

1. Octagon: Located in the Gangnam district, Octagon is one of the most famous and luxurious clubs in Seoul. The club boasts an impressive sound system and attracts both local and international DJs. Entrance fee and drink prices are higher than other clubs, but it's worth the experience for electronic music enthusiasts.

2. NB2: This club in Gangnam is popular among K-pop fans and often hosts celebrity guests. The club plays a mix of K-pop, hip hop, and EDM music and has a lively atmosphere. The club is open until 6 am on weekends, making it a popular spot for party-goers.

3. Contra: Located in Itaewon, Contra is a smaller, intimate club that plays a range of music, from disco to house. The club has a retro vibe and is popular among locals and expats alike. The drinks are reasonably priced, and the dance floor is always packed.

4. Cakeshop: This underground club in Itaewon is known for its underground music scene, with DJs playing a mix of techno, house, and hip hop. The club has a cozy atmosphere and often hosts international artists. The drinks are affordable, and there's a small outdoor terrace for those who want to take a break from the dance floor.

5. Gopchangjeongol: For those who want to experience a traditional Korean drinking culture, Gopchangjeongol is a must-visit spot in Hongdae. The restaurant serves a variety of Korean-style barbecue dishes, and customers can order soju and beer to pair with their food. The restaurant has a lively atmosphere and is a popular spot for groups of friends.

Note that some clubs may have dress codes, and IDs are required to enter most bars and clubs. Additionally, it's important to drink responsibly and stay safe while enjoying Seoul's nightlife scene.

C. Live Music and Performances

Seoul is a city that offers a wide range of live music and performance venues, from small intimate settings to large-scale concert halls. Here are a few notable venues to check out:

1. Blue Note Jazz Club - Located in Gangnam, Blue Note Jazz Club is one of Seoul's premier venues for live jazz music. The club features performances by both local and international jazz artists, with shows held nightly. The venue also offers a full bar and a dinner menu.

Website: https://www.bluenote.co.kr/en/seoul

2. Jamsil Indoor Stadium - Jamsil Indoor Stadium is a large concert venue that has hosted many famous international artists, such as Ed Sheeran, Bruno Mars, and Coldplay. The stadium can hold up to 13,000 people and offers a variety of seating options, from floor seats to balcony seats.

Website: http://www.jamsilarena.co.kr/eng/index.jsp

3. The National Theater of Korea - The National Theater of Korea is a state-run theater that offers a variety of performances, including traditional Korean plays, dance performances, and operas. The theater has three performance halls, with seating for up to 2,500 people.

Website: https://www.ntok.go.kr/en/main.do

4. Club FF - Club FF is a popular venue for live indie music, located in the Hongdae area. The club features performances by up-and-coming local bands and DJs, with shows held most nights of the week. The venue also offers a full bar and a food menu.

Website: https://www.facebook.com/clubffhongdae/

5. Seoul Arts Center - The Seoul Arts Center is a large complex that includes several performance halls, including an opera theater, a concert hall, and a theater for plays and dance performances. The center also hosts art exhibitions and other cultural events throughout the year.

Website: http://www.sac.or.kr/eng/main.jsp

D. Cultural Performances and Shows

Seoul is home to a variety of cultural performances and shows that showcase the country's rich history and traditions. Here are some popular options:

1. Nanta: Nanta is a non-verbal comedy show that incorporates Korean traditional percussion music, known as samulnori. The show features four cooks who prepare a wedding banquet while dealing with a variety of obstacles and mishaps. The energetic performance has become a favorite among both locals and tourists.

Location: Myeongdong Nanta Theatre

Website: http://nanta.i-pmc.co.kr/eng/main/index

2. B-Boy Kung Festival: This festival features high-energy breakdancing performances by some of Korea's top b-boy crews. The festival also includes workshops, competitions, and other events for breakdancing enthusiasts.

Location: Various venues

Website: http://www.bboykung.com/

3. Traditional Korean Music and Dance Performance: This show features traditional Korean music and dance, including performances of court music, folk music, and traditional dance. The performers wear colorful traditional costumes, and the show provides a glimpse into Korea's rich cultural heritage.

Location: Jeongdong Theater

Website: https://www.jeongdong.or.kr/en/main/main.php

4. The Painters: Hero: The Painters: Hero is a performance that combines live painting, music, dance, and multimedia effects. The performers create stunning artworks on stage in real-time, while also telling the story of a hero's journey.

Location: Chungmu Art Hall

Website: https://www.thepainters.co.kr/en/main/main.php

5. Korean Traditional Wedding Ceremony: This performance showcases a traditional Korean wedding ceremony, complete with traditional costumes, music, and dance. The show provides a unique and immersive experience of Korean wedding culture.

Location: Namsangol Hanok Village

Website: http://hanokmaeul.visitseoul.net/en/board/view.do?menu_id=3&board_seq=4327

E. Karaoke Bars

Karaoke, or noraebang as it is called in Korean, is an incredibly popular pastime in South Korea. It is no surprise, then, that Seoul is home to some of the best karaoke bars in the world. Here are some of the best places to belt out your favorite tunes in the city:

1. Coin Noraebang – This chain of karaoke bars is popular among both locals and tourists alike. With over 30 locations throughout Seoul, you are sure to find a Coin Noraebang near your accommodation. The prices are affordable, and the rooms are comfortable and equipped with the latest karaoke machines.

2. Monster Pub – This is a popular spot in the Itaewon neighborhood for karaoke lovers who also enjoy a drink or two. The bar offers an extensive selection of English and Korean songs, as well as private rooms that can accommodate groups of various sizes. The vibe is lively, and the staff is friendly, making it an excellent spot for a fun night out with friends.

3. Melody Karaoke – Located in Gangnam, this karaoke bar is popular among locals for its affordable prices, excellent sound quality, and clean rooms. The staff is attentive and accommodating, and the song selection is extensive, with both Korean and English options.

4. Gao's Karaoke – This is a high-end karaoke bar in the Cheongdam neighborhood of Seoul. The private rooms are luxurious and well-designed, with high-quality audio equipment and mood lighting. The bar also offers a selection of food and drinks, making it an excellent spot for a special occasion or a night out with a group of friends.

5. Noraebar – This karaoke bar is located in the trendy Hongdae neighborhood, popular among university students and young people. It is a fun and lively spot with affordable prices, a wide selection of songs, and private rooms that can accommodate groups of various sizes. The staff is friendly, and the atmosphere is festive, making it an excellent spot for a fun night out with friends.

When visiting any karaoke bar in Seoul, it is important to note that the Korean karaoke culture includes a system where you can order snacks, drinks, and additional time for your room. Be sure to check the prices before ordering, and enjoy your time singing your heart out in one of the world's karaoke capitals.

F. Rooftop Bars

Rooftop bars have become increasingly popular in Seoul over the years, offering a unique drinking and dining experience with stunning city views. Here are some of the best rooftop bars in Seoul:

1. Seoul Pub: Located in the heart of Gangnam, Seoul Pub boasts a beautiful rooftop terrace with breathtaking views of the city. The bar serves a range of beers, cocktails, and food options.

2. The Griffin Bar: Situated in the Itaewon district, The Griffin Bar is known for its relaxed atmosphere and fantastic views of Namsan Tower. The bar offers a variety of drinks, including signature cocktails, and a small selection of snacks.

3. Rooftop Bar at the Westin Chosun: This elegant rooftop bar is located on the 20th floor of the Westin Chosun hotel, offering spectacular views of the city skyline. The bar features a large selection of wines and cocktails, along with a small menu of appetizers and desserts.

4. Maison Glad Rooftop Bar: Located in the Dongdaemun district, this rooftop bar is part of the Maison Glad Hotel and offers panoramic views of the city. The bar serves a range of cocktails and light bites.

5. Floating Rooftop Bar: This unique bar is located on a boat on the Han River, providing a one-of-a-kind experience. The bar offers a variety of drinks and a small selection of food, along with great views of the city and the river.

VIII. Day Trips and Excursions

A. The DMZ and Panmunjom

The DMZ (Demilitarized Zone) is a unique and fascinating destination for visitors to Seoul who are interested in history and politics. The DMZ is a buffer zone between North and South Korea that was established after the Korean War. It is one of the most heavily guarded borders in the world, and visiting the DMZ offers a glimpse into the complex and tense relationship between the two Koreas.

Panmunjom is a small village in the DMZ that is famous for the Joint Security Area (JSA), where North and South Korean soldiers stand face to face. Visitors can enter the JSA and step into North Korea through the blue conference buildings that straddle the border. The experience is both surreal and sobering, as visitors witness firsthand the divided nation and the lingering tensions that continue to affect the Korean peninsula.

To visit the DMZ and Panmunjom, visitors must join a tour with a licensed tour operator. The tour typically includes a visit to Imjingak Park, which is a memorial for the Korean War, and the Dora Observatory, which offers panoramic views of North Korea. The tour also includes a stop at the Third Tunnel of Aggression, a tunnel dug by North Korea to invade the South. Visitors can walk through the tunnel and see the remnants of the explosive devices that were installed by the South Korean military to block it.

It's important to note that visiting the DMZ and Panmunjom requires advanced planning, as there are strict regulations and security procedures in place. Visitors must bring their passport on the day of the tour and follow the instructions of their tour guide at all times.

The DMZ and Panmunjom are located about 50 km north of Seoul and can be accessed by bus or car. The tour typically lasts around 8 hours and can cost around $100-$150 per person. It's recommended to book the tour in advance, especially during peak tourist season.

B. Nami Island

Nami Island, also known as Namiseom Island, is a scenic destination located about an hour and a half away from Seoul. It's a popular day trip for tourists and locals alike, with its beautiful natural scenery and unique attractions.

To get to Nami Island, you can take a shuttle bus or a taxi from the Gapyeong Station, which is accessible by train or subway from Seoul. Alternatively, some tour operators offer package trips that include transportation and admission to the island.

Once you arrive on the island, you'll be greeted by a stunning landscape of trees, gardens, and waterways. Nami Island is especially known for its beautiful tree-lined paths, which are particularly popular during the fall season when the leaves change color.

There are also a variety of activities and attractions on the island, including a zip line, a bike rental, and a miniature train ride. You can also visit the Nami Island International Children's Book Festival, which showcases children's literature from around the world.

One of the most iconic attractions on Nami Island is the statue of the character "Winter Sonata," which was erected in honor of the popular Korean drama filmed on the island. Visitors can take photos with the statue and even visit the "Winter Sonata" exhibit for more information about the show.

In addition to its natural beauty and attractions, Nami Island also offers a variety of dining options, from casual cafes to upscale restaurants. Local delicacies such as grilled chicken skewers and buckwheat noodles are popular choices.

Overall, Nami Island is a must-visit destination for nature lovers and culture enthusiasts alike. Its serene atmosphere and unique attractions make it a perfect escape from the hustle and bustle of Seoul.

C. Suwon Hwaseong Fortress

Suwon Hwaseong Fortress is a UNESCO World Heritage Site and a popular day trip destination from Seoul. The fortress was built in the late 18th century by King Jeongjo as a military stronghold and a royal palace.

Visitors can explore the fortress walls, gates, watchtowers, and pavilions, which offer a glimpse into the architectural and cultural history of the Joseon Dynasty. The fortress covers a vast area of over 5.5 kilometers and is surrounded by a beautiful natural landscape.

One of the main highlights of Suwon Hwaseong Fortress is the Hwaseong Haenggung Palace, a royal palace located inside the fortress walls. The palace features stunning traditional architecture, beautiful gardens, and various exhibits showcasing the daily life of the royal family.

Other popular attractions in the fortress include the Hwaseomun Gate, Janganmun Gate, and Hwahongmun Gate. Visitors can also watch the changing of the guards ceremony, which takes place several times a day.

To get to Suwon Hwaseong Fortress, visitors can take a train from Seoul to Suwon Station, and then transfer to a local bus or taxi to the fortress. The journey takes around an hour, and the fortress is open every day from 9:00 am to 6:00 pm. Admission fees are 3,000 won for adults and 1,500 won for children.

D. Everland Theme Park

Everland is South Korea's largest and most popular theme park, located about an hour's drive from Seoul. It offers a variety of attractions for visitors of all ages, including thrill rides, family-friendly rides, and a zoo.

One of Everland's most popular attractions is T-Express, the world's steepest wooden roller coaster, which offers a thrilling ride through the park's scenic mountainside. Other popular thrill rides include the Hurricane, the Rolling X-Train, and the Double Rock Spin.

For families with young children, there are several areas of the park dedicated to kid-friendly rides and activities. The park's Zootopia section offers a wide range of animal encounters, including a safari ride, petting zoo, and bird sanctuary.

In addition to its rides and attractions, Everland also offers a variety of seasonal events and activities throughout the year, including Halloween-themed events in the fall and a winter festival with a skating rink and illuminated displays during the holiday season.

To get to Everland, visitors can take a shuttle bus from Seoul's Gangnam or Jamsil subway stations or take a public bus from Gangnam or Suwon. Tickets can be purchased online or at the park's entrance, and the park is open daily from 10:00 am to 9:00 pm.

E. Jeonju Hanok Village

Jeonju Hanok Village is a cultural district located in the city of Jeonju, about 2.5 hours south of Seoul by bus or train. The village is a preserved area of traditional Korean houses, called hanok, and provides visitors with a glimpse into Korea's past.

The village is known for its traditional architecture, food, and cultural activities. Visitors can explore the narrow streets and alleys of the village and admire the hanok houses, many of which are over 100 years old. The village is also home to several museums and galleries, showcasing traditional Korean arts and crafts.

One of the main attractions of the village is the Jeonju Hanok Living Experience Center, which offers visitors the opportunity to stay in a hanok house overnight and experience traditional Korean culture firsthand. The center provides various programs, such as tea ceremonies, Korean cooking classes, and hanbok dress-up, for visitors to participate in and learn about Korean culture.

Another popular activity in Jeonju Hanok Village is trying the local cuisine. The village is famous for its bibimbap, a Korean rice dish topped with various vegetables, meat, and a spicy sauce. There are many restaurants and street food vendors throughout the village serving bibimbap and other traditional Korean dishes.

To get to Jeonju Hanok Village from Seoul, visitors can take a bus or train to Jeonju. From the Jeonju bus terminal, there are regular buses to the village, or visitors can take a taxi. The village is also easily accessible by car. It is recommended to spend at least one night in Jeonju to fully explore the village and experience its culture.

IX. Travel Tips and Safety

A. Staying Connected: Wi-Fi and SIM Cards

Staying connected while traveling in Seoul is essential, especially if you need to access maps, communicate with locals, or share your experiences with family and friends. Here's what you need to know about Wi-Fi and SIM cards in Seoul.

Wi-Fi

Seoul offers a variety of Wi-Fi options, including free public Wi-Fi and paid Wi-Fi services. The city's free public Wi-Fi service, known as Seoul Free Wi-Fi, is available in most public areas, including airports, train stations, and tourist attractions. To use the service, you need to register with your email address or social media account.

Many cafes, restaurants, and hotels in Seoul also offer free Wi-Fi for their customers. Look for signs or ask the staff for the Wi-Fi password.

Paid Wi-Fi services are also available in Seoul, including Wi-Fi rental devices and portable Wi-Fi hotspots. These services are convenient if you need a reliable and fast internet connection during your trip. Many companies offer rental services at the airport or online.

SIM Cards

Another option for staying connected in Seoul is to purchase a SIM card for your phone. SIM cards are available at the airport, as well as in many convenience stores and electronics stores throughout the city.

There are several mobile carriers in South Korea, including SK Telecom, KT, and LG U+. You can purchase a prepaid SIM card or a data-only SIM card, depending on your needs. Make sure your phone is unlocked and compatible with the carrier's network before purchasing a SIM card.

B. Etiquette and Cultural Tips

When visiting a foreign country, it's important to be aware of local customs and etiquette to avoid offending anyone or coming across as disrespectful. Here are some etiquette and cultural tips to keep in mind when visiting Seoul:

1. Bowing: Bowing is a common greeting in Korean culture. The depth and duration of the bow will vary depending on the situation and the person you are bowing to. As a visitor, a slight bow of the head or a handshake is usually sufficient.

2. Removing Shoes: It's customary to remove shoes when entering a Korean home or a traditional Korean establishment. Look for a designated shoe storage area or rack and follow the lead of the locals.

3. Chopsticks: Chopsticks are the primary utensil for eating in Korea. Unlike in some other countries, it's not customary to hold the rice bowl up to your mouth or to stab food with chopsticks. Also, avoid pointing with chopsticks or leaving them standing upright in a bowl of rice.

4. Tipping: Tipping is not customary in Korea, and it may even be considered rude in some situations. Instead, service charges are often included in the bill or a small fee may be added to the total cost.

5. Noise Levels: Koreans tend to speak quietly and avoid loud or boisterous behavior in public. Be mindful of your noise level in public spaces like restaurants or on public transportation.

6. Respect for Elders: Respect for elders is deeply ingrained in Korean culture. Addressing elders with appropriate honorifics and showing deference and respect is essential.

7. Dress Code: Seoul is a modern and fashionable city, but it's still important to dress appropriately, especially when visiting religious or traditional sites. Avoid revealing clothing and dress modestly.

8. Punctuality: Being punctual is highly valued in Korean culture, so make sure to arrive on time for appointments, meetings, and tours.

9. Language: While English is widely spoken in tourist areas, it's always helpful to learn a few basic Korean phrases and show an effort to communicate in the local language.

10. Smoking: Smoking is banned in most public spaces in Seoul, including restaurants, cafes, and bars. Be aware of designated smoking areas and avoid smoking in non-designated areas.

C. Emergency Contacts and Useful Apps

In case of an emergency, it's important to have the right contact information and useful apps on hand during your trip to Seoul. Here are some essential contacts and apps to have:

Emergency Contacts:

- Police: 112
- Fire and Ambulance: 119
- Tourist Information Center: +82-2-1330

Useful Apps:

- KakaoMap: This app is a must-have for navigating Seoul's public transportation system. It provides real-time traffic information, public transportation schedules, and directions to destinations.

- KakaoTalk: This messaging app is widely used in South Korea and can be handy for staying in touch with locals or communicating with your travel companions.

- Naver Maps: This app is another popular navigation tool in South Korea and offers detailed maps, public transportation information, and real-time traffic updates.

- Subway Korea: This app provides subway maps and schedules for Seoul and other major cities in South Korea.

- Seoul Bus: This app provides bus schedules and real-time bus location information for Seoul.

It's also a good idea to keep a copy of your passport, travel insurance information, and emergency contact information in a safe place, either in a physical copy or a digital copy on your phone or computer. And always be aware of your surroundings and take basic safety precautions, such as keeping your valuables secure and avoiding unsafe areas at night.

Fun Things to Do in Seoul

Seoul offers a great variety of things to do during your stay: from walking around historical places to night-shopping. Seoul is the city that never sleeps so you will be able to enjoy your time fullest. We have made you a list of recommended tours, however, you are welcomed to explore the city on your own.

Explore Korean Palaces and Traditional Markets

Gyeongbokgung palace main entrance gates

Seoul is well-known for its historical places with beautiful architecture and decorations. Most people start their Seoul journey from visiting at least one of five palaces in Seoul. While touring around palaces you will be able to see a unique Korean architecture, get to know ancient history, see beautiful gardens with ponds and, of course, take majestic photos. This tour also includes Jogyesa Temple – a tranquil place in the middle of the busy city, shopping at traditional markets Insadong filled with craft galleries, souvenir shops and teahouses, and Namdaemun – most famous for its food alley.

This full day tour costs around $83 per person and you can make a booking here http://bit.ly/2IdUgS6. Also, you will get a professional guide that will explain the history and why these places are important to Korean people, and a hotel pick-up and drop off.

Enjoy Night Views of Han River and Namsan Tower

Seoul cityscape from Han River

Seoul is a city that is famous for its night lights as it was selected several times that brightest city in the world. Also, Seoul has amazing parks near the river and stunning Han River cruises where you will be able to enjoy majestic views and try the best food. Another great night views are from Namsan Tower or N Seoul Tower that is located on a Namsan Mountain. This location is very popular between tourists and locals as it offers a great view of Seoul at night.

This 5 hour tour includes Han River cruise with live music and narration, cable car ride to Namsan Tower and hotel pick-up/drop off service. And this spectacular tour costs only $133: http://bit.ly/2Gd9CR2.

Hike Bukhansan Mountain and Experience Traditional Korean Sauna

Seoul can't be experienced without a stunning hike up to Bukhansan Mountain that is basically just around the corner of North Seoul. Bukhansan is the highest mountain in Seoul popular between tourists and locals as it offers great views of Seoul, full of adrenaline hike, historic relics, and gigantic temples. Bukhansan Mountain is very important for Seoul. Are you wondering why? Then book this tour for $121 and your private guide will be able to tell you everything about the mountain and its historic value. Also, this tour includes a Korean sauna – jjimjilbang – experience. You will be able to soak in a hot tube your tired body after the hike. Perfect, isn't it?

You can book this amazing tour here: http://bit.ly/2rD8rFa. This tour is 8 hours tour or longer.

Bukhansan Mountain

Taste Endless Korean Food

Seoul has numerous food markets where you can try traditional Korean street. Namdaemun Market is very famous for its street food that is freshly made by locals. Also, while traveling around Seoul, you have to try Korean BBQ that you cook yourself and wrap into lettuce with some side dishes, rice, and sauces.

Street food at the market

Tour includes street food snacks at Namdaemun, a dish from a local eatery and Korean BBQ experience. For only $83 you will be able to get a never-ending 4 hours of food. Book here: http://bit.ly/2IbUXeJ.

Late Night Shopping in Seoul

Crowded Myeongdong in the evening

Never sleeping Seoul offers lots of locations for shopping and eating. Night markets are getting more and more attention from foreigners. Myeong-dong and Dongdaemun are the most popular shopping streets where you can find branded clothing shops, cheap Korean clothing and lots of makeup stores. Another popular market is Gwangjang market that is famous for its street food, especially for mungbean pancakes.

For $98 you would be able to get food tasting, a local guide that will help you with your shopping and discounts, hotel pick up and drop off service, and a great time. If you are interested, book this tour here: http://bit.ly/2IzXv5N.

Gorgeous Photoshoot in Hanbok

We perfectly know that the majority of people like taking photos especially when they travel. If you are traveling around Seoul, you must have noticed people wearing colorful dresses from ancient times. These dresses are called hanbok and it is traditional Korean clothes that can be rented from various places around palaces. If you want to take great photos with hanbok, think about booking this tour from http://bit.ly/2IcIgAt for $69. This tour enables you to select a unique colored hanbok from popular hanbok rental shop and wear it for 4 hours while taking photos at palaces or hanok village.

Beautiful hanboks at the rental store

Seoul Mountains: Bukhansan National Park Including Temples and Seoul Fortress Wall

Seoul is one of the most modern cities in the world that is filled with traditional buildings and surrounded by more than 36 mountains. A visit to Seoul without experiencing hiking the most beautiful mountains is not complete. Here we are going to introduce you to breathtaking Seoul hikes and what you need to know about them.

Bukhansan National Park

Bukhansan National Park is located in the north of Seoul and Gyeonggi region covering an area of 79.92 square kilometers. The park was established in 1983 and its name means 'north Han (river) mountain'. Bukhansan National Park is the only one South Korea's national park that is located within the city and easily accessible by public transport. Every year more than 5 mln hikers visit a national park.

Most famous mountains of the national park are Bukhansan Baegundae Peak and Dobongsan Jaunbong. However, if you aren't interested in hiking the highest peaks, you can always choose any other trail of 98 trails.

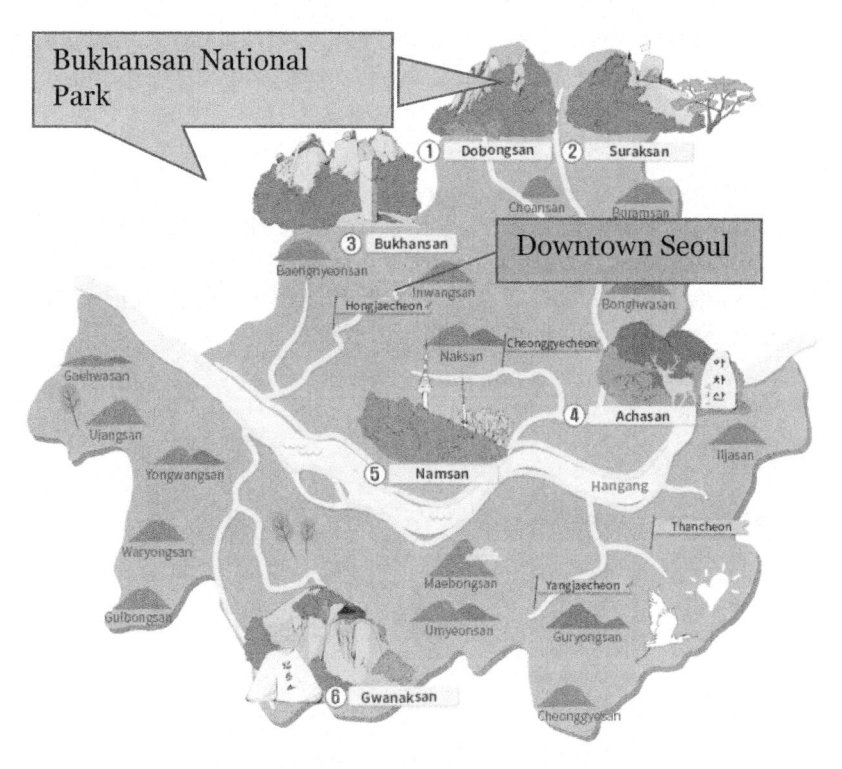

Location of Bukhansan National Park compared to other mountains in Seoul

Which Temples to Visit

Bukhansan National Park has more than 100 temples and monk cells so we have made a simple list of worth visiting temples for your first hike.

- **Guknyeongsa Temple**

This is a Buddhist temple and is famous for its giant golden Buddha statue. It takes only 45 minutes from the mountain entrance and is on the way if you are hiking Baegundae Peak at Bukhansan Mountain.

- **Dobogsa Temple**

This temple is a perfect stopover if you are hiking Jaunbong Peak at Dobongsan Mountain. You won't need to hike much as Dobongsa temple is located on a foot of the mountain. Dobongsa temple is quite modern, medium-sized and has souvenir and snack shop. Perfect if you want to buy a souvenir from a temple. Also, if you visit

Dobongsa temple during summer and early autumn, you will be impressed by gorgeous blooming flowers around the temple.

- **Cheonchuksa Temple**

Another great temple on a way to Jaunbong Peak at Dobongsan Mountain. You will need to leave your hiking path and hike another way in order to reach the temple. Little side hike is worth as you will see the majestic view of numerous rows of Budha stone statues. Also, you can visit temple buildings and have fresh water.

Map of Temples

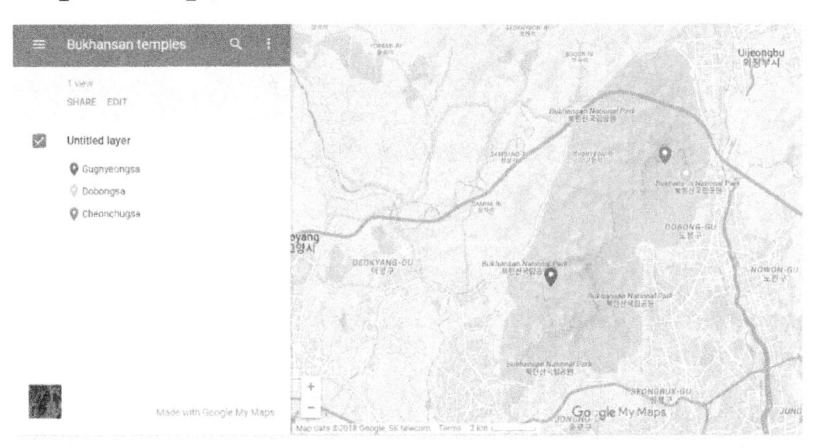

Get the full Google map here http://bit.ly/2rMMm8h

Reasons to Visit Bukhansan National Park

The majority of Koreans love hiking and spending their time in nature as Seoul is always a noisy and busy city that tires everyone. If you are still skeptical about getting tired of Seoul, take a look at your top reasons why you need to visit Bukhansan National Park.

1. Escape from loud and busy city life in order to feel like you have your own personal space.
2. Enjoy best views of Seoul from above.
3. Make some friends. Korean people are more open and friendly during the hike, so you will easily find several people to talk to.
4. Get stunning photos. If you like taking photos, you will fall in love with mountains and temples that can be a perfect background for your 'photoshoot'.

5. Experience Korean culture. Mountains hold a very important meaning to Korean history as there are an old fortress wall and tons of secret gates.

Seoul Fortress Wall Hike

Seoul Fortress Wall is a former fortress wall that runs around downtown Seoul and is included in Historic Site in South Korea list. The wall is 18.6 kilometers long and connects four mountains: Inwangsan, Baegaksan/Bugaksan, Naksan, and Namsan. Seoul Fortress Wall was initially built in 1396 and it took 98 days. During the Japanese occupation, the majority of the fortress wall was destroyed and some of the parts were recently (2014) rebuilt. Seoul Government is still working on completely reconstructing the wall and its gates.

Location of Seoul Fortress Wall

Even though Seoul Fortress Wall is basically located in downtown Seoul, you won't be able to spot the wall very easily as most of the parts in the main streets aren't reconstructed. However, you will notice huge ancient gates standing in the middle of busy roads – they are part of the wall. The most visible parts of the fortress wall are in the mountains.

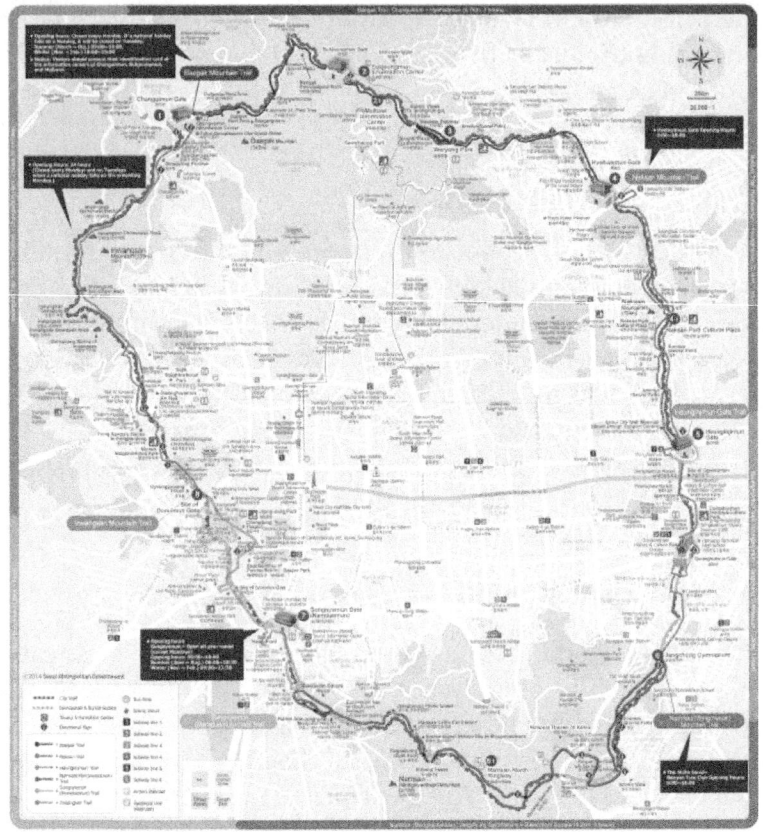

Map of Seoul Fortress Wall, get full one here: http://bit.ly/2InRHJf

A Short Guide to Walking Trails

Bugaksan/Baegaksan Mountain Trail

Name: Changuimun Gate – Hyehwamun Gate| **Distance**: 4.7 km| **Duration:** ~3 hours

This short trail runs across the mountain Bugaksan (342 m) which is one of the inner mountains of old Seoul and is the highest one. Until 2007 access to the mountain was closed to the public as the reason of North Korean Special Forces infiltration in Seoul in 1968. Even though now it's open for public, there are some restrictions regarding the trail such as it's closed on Mondays, opened at 9:00 to 16:00, and every visitor have to fill the visiting form and have an ID in order to hike a mountain. Also, you need to finish hike by a certain time and you have to take in mind that during a hike you will be watched by tons of army guys and won't be allowed to take photos in certain spots.

More detailed information about what you will be able to see during this hike and a closed up map is here:
http://seoulcitywall.seoul.go.kr/front/eng/sub04/sub0401.do

Naksan Mountain Trail| Name: Hyehwamun Gate – Heunginjimun Gate| Distance: 2.1 km, Duration: ~1 hr

This trail is a very short trail that can be combined with other Seoul Fortress Wall trails if you wish to do more walking. The trail leads via Naksan Mountain (124 m) and the mural village of Ihwa-dong. You will be able to see the bohemian neighborhood filled with impressive views of Seoul. This trail is very famous for watching sunset and sunrise. More information here
http://seoulcitywall.seoul.go.kr/front/eng/sub04/sub0401.do
if you scroll down and click Naksan trail section.

Heunginjimun Gate Trail

Name: Heunginjimun Gate – Jangchung Gymnasium| Distance: 1.8 km| Duration: ~1 hr

Another short trail that can be easily combined with another trail. This trail leads through almost completely destroyed Seoul Fortress Wall area and is recommended to visit Dongdaemun Design Plaza (DDP), Dongdaemun and Pyeonghwa markets while walking on this trail. If you more information about the trail, scroll down and press Heunginjimun Gate Trail
http://seoulcitywall.seoul.go.kr/front/eng/sub04/sub0401.do

Namsan Mountain Trail

Name: Jangchung Gymnasium – Baekbeom Square| Distance: 4.2 km| Duration: ~3 hrs

This trail leads through Jangchung neighborhood across Namsan Mountain (270 m) that is considered to be a 'central point of Seoul'. Most of the wall was destroyed in 1920s during Japanese occupation, however Seoul Government working on rebuilding the wall. The majority of the wall has been rebuilt, however, there is no exact date when the rest of the wall will be finished. If you go on this trail, you will be able to see the famous Seoul N Tower that is a popular location for couples. We recommend walking this trail during the evening for the beautiful lights of Seoul. Scroll down and press Namsan Mountain Trail for more information at this website: http://seoulcitywall.seoul.go.kr/front/eng/sub04/sub0401.do

Sungnyemun Gate Trail

Name: Baekbeom Square – Site of Donuimun Gate| Distance: 1.8 km| Duration: ~1 hr

This part of the Seoul Fortress Wall is completely destroyed and only gate or memorial plate of the site is left. Due to this reason, you might need a guide or very detailed map in order to keep with a fortress wall trail. The most famous part of this trail is Sungnyemun Gate (Namdaemun Gate) that is located next to Namdaemun market, so you will be able to have a few snacks at this traditional market while being on a trail. For more information visit website and scroll down to find a Sungnyemun Trail http://seoulcitywall.seoul.go.kr/front/eng/sub04/sub0401.do

Inwangsan Mountain Trail

Name: Site of Donuimun Gate – Changuimun Gate| Distance: 4 km| **Duration:** ~2 hrs 30 min

Another hiking trail that leads across Inwangsan Mountain (339 m). Inwangsan is famous for its rock formations, especially the meditation rock – Seonbawi, and a Buddhist temple. Due to the North Korean invasion in 1968, Inwangsan trail was closed for public till 1993. Now is easily accessible but monitored by Korean Special Forces. Take into your mind that trail is closed on Mondays and on Tuesdays when the national holiday is on Monday. Also, you have to take extra care if you are hiking on a rainy day or winter. Scroll down, find Inwangsan Mountain trail for more information http://seoulcitywall.seoul.go.kr/front/eng/sub04/sub0401.do

Map of Important Areas to Visit on Seoul Fortress Wall

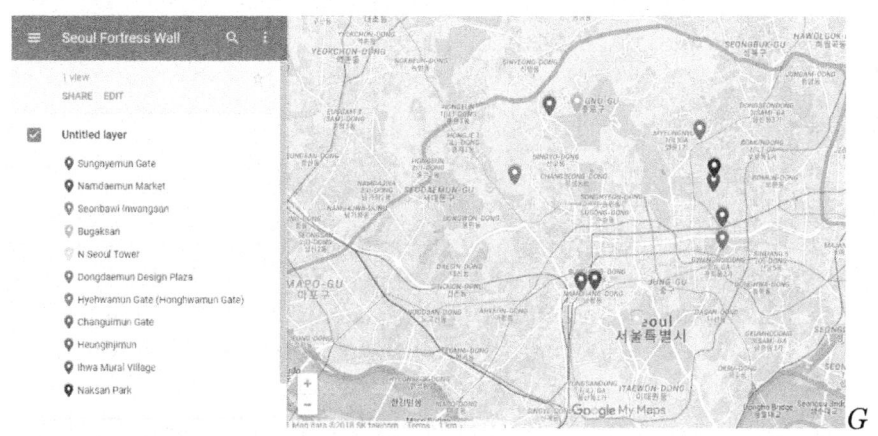

Get the full map here http://bit.ly/2rKhc1o

3-Day Seoul Classic Travel Itinerary

1ˢᵗ Day in Seoul: Arrival, Exploring Neighborhood, Palaces, Insadong and Top Restaurants in Jongno-gu

7:15am. Arrival at Incheon International Airport.

Most international flights are to and from Incheon Airport that is just outside Seoul. Always try to get a morning flight as it will give you more time to explore the city. Incheon Airport is quite big so you can be easily distracted by various duty-free and souvenir shops, and live performances. Despite being big, it has two terminals and is very well marked and you can easily find tourists information center.

7:30 am. Immigration and Luggage.

Upon arrival at Incheon Airport, take the shuttle subway to the Passport Control zone. You will be directed to a line for foreigners, where airport volunteers will assist you with your documents and any questions you may have. At the Passport Control desk, present your ID and flight card, look at the camera, and place your fingers on the scanner. Once cleared, proceed to the baggage claim area and remember to take note of your luggage gate number for quicker retrieval.

7:45 am. Use the provided map of Incheon Airport transportation and hail a standard taxi to your guesthouse, Bukchonmaru, located in the Bukchon Hanok Village. The double room with a shared bathroom costs $90 per night. The journey from the airport to the guesthouse takes around 40 minutes.

Bukchon Hanok Village is a wealthy neighborhood situated between two palaces and famous streets like Insadong and Samcheongdong. The name Bukchon translates to 'northern village' and was once the residence of aristocrats, officials, and scholars during the Joseon Dynasty (1392-1910). The village is home to over hundreds of traditional Korean houses called hanoks, with many now converted into galleries, tea rooms, guesthouses, and restaurants. There are still people who live in hanoks in the village, preserving its rich history and culture.8:25 am. Check in your guesthouse.

Upon arrival at your guesthouse at 8:25 am, check in and freshen up by changing your clothes. Once settled, head to the kitchen to enjoy a delicious traditional Korean breakfast provided by the hospitable Bukchonmaru hosts. This filling meal will give you plenty of energy to last at least half a day of exploring the city.

8:50 am. At 8:50 am, take your time after breakfast and prepare to leave the guesthouse. Grab your map and head in the direction of Gyeongbokgung Palace. There's no need to rush, take your time and enjoy the journey.

The neighborhood of Bukchon Hanok village

As you make your way towards Bukchon Hanok Village, take some time to explore the luxurious area of Samcheongdong. This neighborhood is situated between Gyeongbokgung Palace and Bukchon Hanok Village and is known for its upscale hanok restaurants, coffee shops, tea houses, boutiques, shops, and art galleries. The area is a beautiful blend of traditionalism and modernism, with many of the buildings being hanoks mixed with modern structures. Be sure to take some photos and soak in the luxurious atmosphere of Samcheongdong before continuing on to Bukchon Hanok Village.

At 9:45 am, you will arrive at Gyeongbokgung Palace. Since the palace opens at 9 am, you will be among the first visitors. To enter Gyeongbokgung Palace, you will need to purchase a ticket. There are two types of tickets available - a $3 ticket that includes entry to only Gyeongbokgung Palace or a $10 ticket that includes entrance to all 5 palaces and Jongmyo Shrine.

Note that this itinerary includes only one palace, but if you have more time, you can visit other palaces as well. Gyeongbokgung Palace is the largest palace in Seoul and was originally built in 1395. Its name means 'palace greatly blessed by Heaven' and it is surrounded by four inner Seoul mountains - Inwangsan, Bugaksan, Naksan, and Namsan.

Although the palace was completely destroyed in the late 16th century, it was rebuilt in the 19th century. During the Japanese rule, many parts of Gyeongbokgung were destroyed, and a large government building was constructed in front of the main palace gates. The Korean War further damaged the palace, but as of 2018, about half of the original buildings have been restored. However, since the Seoul Government is still working on the restoration, some parts of the palace may be closed during your visit.

Hyangwonjeong Pavilion in the courtyard of Gyeongbokgung

There are two museums in the palace: the National Palace Museum and the National Folk Museum of Korea. They are both free to visit.

11.40am. Head to **Gwanghwamun Square** located in front of the palace.

Opened in 2009, Gwanghwamun Square is a bustling center of Seoul. Located in the middle of a busy road, the square is home to two famous statues - one of King Sejong and the other of Admiral Yi

Sun Shin. Additionally, there is a modern underground museum dedicated to these two historic figures. If museums are not your thing, take a stroll through the underground passages that connect many buildings in Gwanghwamun, creating an almost underground town.

Gwanghwamun Square: Back of Admiral Yi Sun Shin statue

12:20pm. Leave Gwanghwamun Square and head towards **Insadong**. Get your map read as it's tricky. Make sure you see a **Gwanghwamun Station Exit 2** in the direction you are going.

12:35 pm. Arrival to Insadong.

Insadong is a neighborhood where you can find everything related to Korean culture. You can purchase hanbok (traditional clothes), hanji (traditional paper), traditional teas, pottery, and other crafts.

12:50pm. Insadong is the perfect place to eat. We recommend getting your first lunch in Seoul here. Restaurant **Sanchon** (http://bit.ly/2wSbEGT) is the most famous for its traditional Korean temple cuisine. The restaurant is set as a temple and serve only vegetarian food. The usual price for the course is around $45. It's pricey but you get a great atmosphere.

13:40pm. Relax with a tea at Shin Old Tea House.

Teahouse is in the alley and very well marked so it will be very easy to find. It is a traditional tea house and you will have to sit on the floor. We highly recommend ordering a plum tea as it goes really well with rice cakes.

14:15pm. Start leaving Insadong and head **towards Changdeokgung.** If you have decided to leave earlier, on your way to Changdeokgung you can visit **Unhyeongung (Royal Residence).** It's **free** admission and very small.

14:45pm. Entrance to Changdeokgung Palace and Huwon (Secret Garden). Entrance fee is 3000 won ($3) for the palace and 8000 won ($8) for a guided tour to Secret Garden. You can use your combined palaces ticket and separately buy Secret Garden ticket.

15:00pm. Guided tour to Secret Garden (Huwon)

The Secret Garden, located at the rear of the palace, was exclusively used by the royal family and covers about 60% of the palace grounds. King Taejong (1400-1418) built it for his family to use for rest, writing, and reading. It is said that the garden was meant to be a natural haven, untouched by human intervention, and is home to trees that are more than 300 years old.

Hourly Huwon tours are available, with guides who speak several languages at no extra charge. If you do not specify a language preference, you will automatically be placed in the English guided tour.

One of the rest areas with a pond in Huwon (Secret Garden), Changdeokgung Palace

16:30 pm. Explore Changdeokgung Palace.

Changdeokgung Palace is the second largest palace in Seoul and is included in UNESCO World Heritage List. The palace was built during King Taejong (1400-1418) reign and after Gyeongbokgung destruction served as the main palace till the 19th century. Changdeokgung Palace is more delicate and represents woman as it is said that King Taejong built this palace for his queen. There numerous little gates, chambers and little gardens around the palace.

Opening times for Changdeokgung: Feb-May; Sept-Oct: 9:00-18:00| Jun-Aug: 9:00-18:30| Nov-Jan: 9:00-17:30

Last admission is one hour before closing time. If you are visiting during National Holiday, entrance to the palace is free. Also, during summer and early autumn, Changdeokgung is open for a night tour, just ask at the ticket booth.

Chinese Juniper at Changdeokgung is more than 750 years old

18:25pm. Subway to Tosokchon restaurant.

Take a subway from Anguk station to Gyeongbokgung station. Traveling time: 7 minutes + 5 minutes walking to the restaurant. Subway fare: 1250 won ($1.25).

18:45pm. Dinner at Tosokchon restaurant.

This restaurant is famous for its steamed chicken ginger soup called Samgyetang. Be prepared to wait in a queue as Tosokchon is very popular between locals and foreigners. Also, it's a hanok style restaurant, so prepare to sit on a floor.

20:45pm. Wander around Seochon.

Seochon means 'west village' as it is located west of Gyeongbokgung and is the oldest Jongno neighborhood. There are numerous alleys filled with hanok style shops and restaurants standing next to stylish modern buildings. Seochon alleys resemble cozy maze as modern spaces are well balanced with Korea's tradition.

Alley in Seochon

21:55pm. Subway to the guesthouse.

Gyeongbokgung station line 3 to Anguk station line 3. Travel time: 7 minutes + 15 minutes walking to Bukchonmaru guesthouse. Fare: 1250 won ($1.25). While walking back to guesthouse use Naver maps or follow signs of Bukchon Hanok Village/Junang Middle School/Gahoe-dong.

22:20pm. Arrive at Bukchonmaru guesthouse.

Map of all locations from the 1st day

Get the full map here: *http://bit.ly/2KzHFp2*

2nd Day in Seoul: Seoul Fortress Wall – Inwangsan, Bugaksan, Naksan Including Hyehwa-dong, Ihwa Mural Village and Shopping at Dongdaemun

7:00 am. Wake up and get ready for breakfast. Today is going to be a hard and long full of excitement day.

7:30 am. Eat **breakfast** at your guesthouse and prepare to set off. Wear comfortable shoes and clothes in order to be able to do some hiking. You can pack a spare set of clothes for the evening. Don't forget a water bottle.

7:50 am. Arrive at **Anguk Station** and take the subway to Dongnimmun Station line 3. Journey time: 9 minutes. Fare: 1250 won ($1.25).

8:00 am. Find the nearest **convenience store** like **7eleven (7/11)** or **GS25**, and buy some snack to last for several hours while hiking.

Start following signs of Seoul Fortress Wall and Hyundai Apartments, from apartments take a straight road up till you see a red and green colored gate. **Note!** Look at the map if you can't see any signage or ask people from a convenience store.

107

Gates marking the entrance of Inwangsan

8:20 am. Arrive at Guksadang.

Guksadang is a shamanist shrine that is said to be the most important shrine for rituals performed by shamans. It is believed that Guksadang shrine was first established in 1395. Look around the shrine and continue hiking.

8:40 am. Seonbawi Rock.

Steep stairs will lead you to Seonbawi (Zen/Mediation) rock. It's a very popular spot for praying, so be quiet and respectful.

8:50 am. Follow the Seoul Fortress Wall. Behind the rock, you will see a Seoul Fortress Wall, keep following it. Little by little you will start going up through the rocks. Even though it's easy to hike, be careful as rocks are quite slippery.

View from Inwangsan

Keep following the signs of Changuimun in order to finish the first trail of the Seoul Fortress Wall path. Take into mind that you will see an army lookout towers and soldiers. Also, you won't be able to take photos in certain spots for the security reasons.

10:05 am. Arrive at Changuimun and take a break. Don't worry if you are a little bit early or late. Go to the Bugaksan office and get a registration form. Fill all your passport details and where you are staying.

Bukchonmaru address: 152 Changdeokgung-gil (2-164 Gye-dong), Seoul, SO, South Korea

Bukchonmaru phone number: 01032538751

Hand in your application and you will be given a number. You have to return the visitor card and be off the mountain around 3 pm. Take in mind that Bugaksan is higher and more difficult to hike as there are numerous steps.

Changuimun Gates – one of fortress mini gates that is still standing up to these days

10:15 am. Start hiking. Just simply follow signs for Seoul Fortress Wall and hike along fortress wall for the whole time.

The Bugaksan front looks down to Blue House (Korea's Presidential House) and downtown Seoul, and it offers a great view of majestic Seoul. There is a famous 121 bullet tree that is related to the 1968 North Korean invasion to the Blue House as the tree took the bullets during the conflict. Unfortunately, you aren't permitted to take any photos of downtown Seoul for security reasons so you won't be able to capture a perfect view of the Blue House and palaces beneath the mountain. Also, Bugaksan is a highly militarized area, so you will be watched all the time.

12:30 pm. Arrive at Waryong Park.

Waryong Park is located on the roof of Bugaksan, near Samcheong Park. Head straight through the park towards Ammun (Secret Path)/ Seoul Science High School. Follow the Seoul Fortress Wall/Ammun/Seoul Science High School or Hyehwamun signs. You will see beautiful blossoming flowers, grand trees and lots of people enjoying outdoor sports.

13:10pm. Hyehwamun Gate and Hyehwa-dong.

Hyehwamun, also known as Honghwamun, was originally built in 1396 and served as one of eight city wall gates leading to northern Seoul.

During the Japanese occupation period in 1928 Hyehwamun was destroyed in order to make space for a streetcar line. The gate was rebuilt in 1992 and became a popular spot for students.

Now Hyehwamun is located in a popular area called Hyehwadong with lots of nice coffee shops, restaurants, shops, and murals. Gate's steps are open from 9:00 to 18:00.

View of Hyehwamun from the steps.

13:50pm. Lunch at Masizzim.

The restaurant is located near Hyehwa station that is about 3-5 minutes walk from Hyehwamun.

Masizzim serves traditional Korean stews. You can select pork or beef ribs and they come together with lots of vegetables, nice thick broth and boiling hot accompanied with numerous plates of side dishes. Perfect lunch after all day hike.

15:25pm. Refreshing drink at Hakrim Dabang.

Opened in 1956 and is the oldest traditional coffee house in Seoul. Back the day it was a popular spot for students to meet and discuss protests for their rights. Nowadays, it's a quiet spot for relaxing with vintage books, vinyl records, and black and white photographs.

You can get a nice house blended coffee, various teas, and homemade lemonade. Also, definitely try the famous cream cheesecake.

16:35 pm. Ihwa Mural Village.

Ihwa Mural Village is close to Naksan park, so you have to follow directions of the park. Ihwa-dong back in 1965-1987 was a popular area for teenagers' gatherings after school. Today, Ihwa neighborhood is filled with colorful murals that make a perfect spot for photos. Wander around the alleys and explore this beautiful rural village. Be ready to hike as alleys are quite steep. **Note!** Don't forget to be respectful of residence and only come through the gates and doors if there is a sign 'enter/come in'.

18:45pm. Sunset at Naksan Park.

While exploring Ihwa Mural Village, you will find signs for Naksan Park. Keep following them and you will enter Naksan Park and will see a Seoul Fortress Wall again. Naksan Park is well-known for its night view of Seoul. As you walk across the park, you can enjoy spectacular views.

Night view of Seoul from Naksan Park

19:20pm. Dongdaemun Gate and Gwangjang Market.

Dongdaemun is located just across Naksan Park and is connected via Dongdaemun Fortress Park. Dongdaemun is named after Dongdaemun (Heunginjimun) Gate meaning 'big east gate'. Also, the most fascinating thing about Dongdaemun is that it is standing in the middle of busy roads and has a small wall at the back of the gate that reflects late Joseon Dynasty architecture. Perfect spot for night photography.

If you fancy a late snack, head to Gwangjang Market. It's a popular place for Korean street and is the oldest market in all of South Korea. You must try a plate of sundae (blood sausage with mung bean noodles) served with some steamed lung, perilla leaf, and chili salt. Another must-try food is bindaeddeok (mung bean pancake) served with soy sauce and pickled onions. Prices vary from 3000 won ($3) to 10 000 won ($10).

21:00pm. Shopping at Dongdaemun.

Dongdaemun area is famous for shopping as there are many department stores, clothing market, wholesaler stores, and high-end designer stores. After your tiring day head to Migliore Department Store known for fashionable Korean clothes. You can't try any clothes and most of the vendors don't accept returns, so be thoughtful before you buy. Also, cash is the best as you will be able to get a discount. If you can't find anything you like, try Dongdaemun Night Market that is just next to Migliore. You can't try clothes, use cash to get a discount and if you buy something in bulk, you will get freebies.

22:15pm. Cheonggyecheon walk.

Cheonggyecheon path leading to downtown of Seoul from Dongdaemun

Cheonggyecheon is the stream that goes across downtown Seoul. Before 2005 Cheonggyecheon was neglected and hidden by an overpass, and now it is a most popular location to relax in the middle of Seoul. Cheonggyecheon is crowded during daytime and nighttime equally. As you walk along the stream, you will notice beautiful bridges and popular tourists destinations such as Insadong, palaces and Cheonggye Plaza. Relax your mind and enjoy the beauty of night Seoul.

Note! Seoul is an extremely safe city and Cheonggyecheon path is well lighted with policemen walking along the stream. If you visiting during winter, it's not recommended to take this long walk.

Finish your walk at Cheonggye Plaza near City Hall.

23:20pm. Cheonggye Plaza.

Cheonggye Plaza is a starting point of Cheonggyecheon. There are artificial falls, light installments, and art around the plaza. Also, sometimes festivals like lantern festival or arts festival happening there.

00:00am. Return to guesthouse and rest.

Map of 2nd-day locations

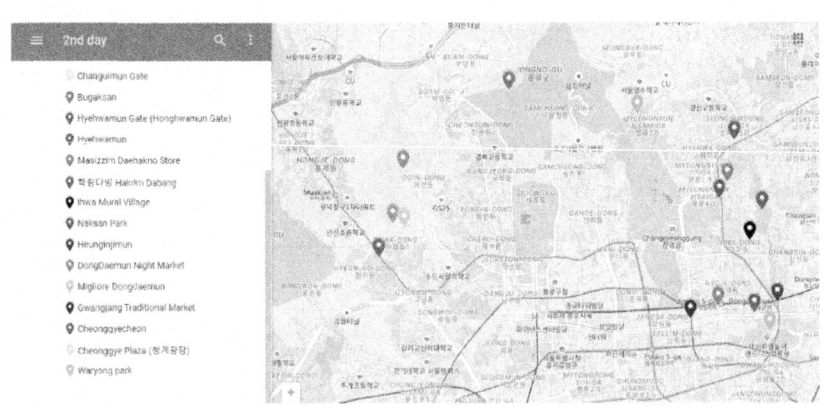

Get the full Google map here: *http://bit.ly/2IQLvNB*

3rd Day in Seoul: Yeouido Park, Han River Cruise, Banpo Han River Park, Bongeunsa Temple, and Departure

8:00 am. Breakfast at the guesthouse.

8:40 am. Check out from the guesthouse. Ask for guesthouse owners to arrange you a **luggage drop off at Incheon Airport** at the time of your flight.

9:30 am. Arrive at Gwanghwamun station line 5. You have to take this line to go to Yeouinaru station which is located on the other side of the river. You are heading to Yeouinaru to take a Han River cruise. Journey time on the subway: 14 minutes. Fare: 1250 won ($1.25).

9:55 am. Arrive at E-Land Han River Cruise port. The Han River cruise ticket booths start operating from 10 am so you will have several minutes to get some snacks from a convenience store and take a look at the morning river.

One of Han River parks

10:05 am. E-Land Han River Cruise Tickets.

E-Land Han River Cruise started operating in 1986 in order to showcase the natural beauty of Seoul. Also, it aims to promote the Han River as a tourists' attraction for foreign visitors. E-Land currently has two terminals and 7 docks: Yeouido, Jamsil, Ttukseom, Jamdubong, Seonyudo, Seoul Forest, Gimpo, and Incheon.

More information about cruise types and prices here: http://bit.ly/2KI5taC

We recommend taking a Daytime River Cruise that starts at 11:30.

10:15 am. Yeouido Han River Park

Yeouido Han River Park is one of the most famous parks along the river. You can enjoy great views of north Seoul, see some sculptures and famous 63 Building that was Korea's first tallest building. Perfect place to spend your time while waiting for your cruise.

Yeouido Han River Park

11:30 am. Han River Cruise.

Take the Han River Cruise. The route of the cruise is Yeouido – Seogangdaegyo – Yeouido and it takes around 40 minutes. There is a seagull feeding add-on option, so you will be able to enjoy the company of seagulls. Also, a professional guide is going to tell you all about the Han River: its story and importance to Korean people.

12:15pm. Take a subway from **Yeouinaru station line 5 to Express Bus Terminal Station line 9.** You will need to transfer at Yeouido station line 5 to line 9. Journey time will be around 31 minutes. Fare: 1250 won ($1.25).

12:46 pm. Express Bus Terminal. Get out of the station and head towards Banpo Bridge. It's a short and well-marked walk.

13:05. Banpo Bridge and Han River Park.

Banpo Han River Park and Banpo Bridge is located between Hannam and Dongjak Bridge and is the most famous bridge in Seoul. It connects southern Seoul (Gangnam) and northern Seoul (Yongsan). Banpo Bridge has inbuilt rainbow fountains on both sides that operate during late spring to early fall evening time.

Banpo Han River Park is popular for various entertainment facilities, beautiful landscape and artificial floating islands that provides various leisure facilities for locals such as restaurants, water bike rides and etc.

Floating Island at night and Banpo Bridge in the background

13:25pm. Chimaek picnic.

Chimaek is chicken + beer combination that is usually delivered by various fried chicken restaurants. You can get fried chicken and beer from vendors in Banpo Han River Park. However, we strongly recommend you to 'catch' a delivery guy (they usually delivering orders around the park) and order straight from him as ordering by phone would be more complicated. Delivery guys usually speak English, so you won't get too much problem. The fried chicken is from various Korean fast food restaurants, so don't expect to get KFC.

Prices vary but you should be ready to pay around 10 000 to 15 000 won ($10-$15) for chicken pieces with beer. If you don't drink beer, get a soft drink.

13:50pm. Take a subway from Express Bus Terminal Station to Cheongdam Station line 9. Fare: 1250 won ($1.25)

14:10pm. Arrive at Bongeunsa Temple near COEX

Bongeunsa temple is located in the busiest part of the Gangnam district, north of enormous shopping and leisure center COEX. The temple was built in 794 and it got refurbished in 1498.

It's the biggest temple that can be found in Seoul. Bongeunsa has 3479 Buddhist scriptures and giant stone Buddha that perfectly fits within Gangnam tall buildings.

Temple is free to enter and is open all the time.

Bongeunsa Temple buildings and Gangnam skyscrapers in the background

15:20pm. Take a taxi to **Incheon International Airport**. Journey time: around 51 minutes. Length of journey: 68.45 km.

Another option:

From Bongeunsa station line 9 take the subway to Gimpo Airport line 9 (1 hr 3 minutes) and transfer at Gimpo Airport to AREX line going towards Incheon Airport (40 minutes). Fare: 4250 won ($4.25).

Map of 3rd Day Locations

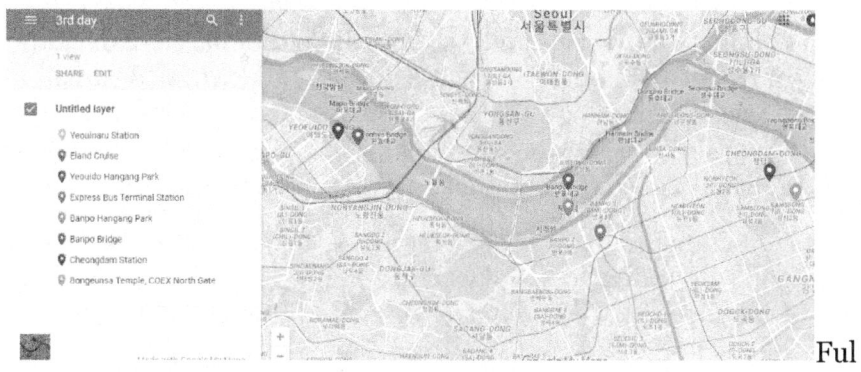

Full map online: *http://bit.ly/2wYQWoR*

Thank you

Thank you for reading this travel guide to Seoul, South Korea! We hope that this guide has provided you with valuable information about accommodations, sightseeing, shopping, dining, nightlife, day trips, and travel tips for your upcoming trip to Seoul.

Seoul is a city that seamlessly blends traditional Korean culture with modern amenities, making it a unique and exciting destination for travelers of all kinds. From exploring ancient palaces and temples to shopping at trendy boutiques and indulging in delicious Korean cuisine, there is something for everyone in Seoul.

Remember to pack comfortable shoes and dress for the weather, as you will be doing a lot of walking and exploring. Don't be afraid to try new things and immerse yourself in Korean culture, and most importantly, have fun and enjoy your trip to Seoul!

Printed in Great Britain
by Amazon